Six Moquette Row

Six Moquette Row

*The Tragedies and Triumphs
of the Sullivan Family*

John F. Sullivan

SIX MOQUETTE ROW
THE TRAGEDIES AND TRIUMPHS OF THE SULLIVAN FAMILY

iUniverse books may be ordered through booksellers or by contacting:

iUniverse LLC
1663 Liberty Drive
Bloomington, IN 47403
www.iuniverse.com
1-800-Authors (1-800-288-4677)

ISBN: 978-1-4917-4519-9 (sc)
ISBN: 978-1-4917-4516-8 (e)

Library of Congress Control Number: 2014916228

Printed in the United States of America.

iUniverse rev. date: 10/02/2014

Dedication

This book is dedicated to Sr. Gloria Sullivan, O.S.U., who is, without dispute, the unofficial genealogist and inspirational leader of the Sullivan/Carroll *blended* family.

Sr. Gloria's wit, tolerance, incredible memory and, above all, her love of family has been a sustaining force in preserving the memory and accomplishments of this remarkable family. For decades, she has been the conduit among the descendants of the blended family, keeping each family unit informed of the happening of the others. Relatives who have never met, know each other because of her ability to keep communication lines opened.

Sr. Gloria has been the inspirational force behind the writing of this book. Thus, it is with great honor that it is dedicated to her. It is hoped that the respect and love of family that Gloria Sullivan has instilled in all of us will continue to inspire future branches of the blended family tree.

Contents

Foreword

What's in a Name?

Unearthing the origin of the name *Sullivan* is a daunting task, tantamount to first finding the haystack, then finding the needle. A combination of fact, myth, and Irish folklore makes it extremely difficult to separate truth from fiction since all stories seem to combine a healthy combination of both. Present-day Sullivans, who are searching for lost family treasure, would be better served chasing that allusive leprechaun with his legendary pot of gold. For the Sullivans, lost wealth is all part of the myth.

What does exist is a story of strife, perseverance, determination and pride. Beginning around 1600 BC a Celtic tribe landed on the Beara Peninsula in the southwestern part of Ireland believed to be the Province of Munster, in which the County of Tipperary is located. Throughout this early Irish historical period, the Sullivans established themselves as warriors, adapting a motto which, roughly translated, means *The Steady Hand of Victory*. Their claim of Irish nobility is based on the fact that they are descendants of Finghin, who was the King of Munster around 620 A.D.

According to Wikipedia, "The O'Sullivans are the medieval and modern continuation of the ancient <u>Eóganacht Chaisil</u> sept of Cenél Fíngin, being descendants of <u>Fíngen mac Áedo Duib</u>, king of <u>Cashel</u> or <u>Munster</u> from 601 to 618. They are thus understood to be of royal extraction. <u>Fedelmid mac Crimthainn</u> (died 847), the celebrated <u>King of Munster</u> and <u>High King of Ireland</u>, was the last king of the Cenél Fíngin/O'Sullivan line. Later they became the chief princes underneath their close kinsmen, the <u>MacCarthy Dynasty</u>, in a small, but powerful <u>Kingdom of Desmond</u>, successor of Cashel/Munster (Cashel is a town in Tipperary)."

The Sullivans are believed to be descendants of one person and thus are, in one way, or another, all related through a common blood line. The Irish surname Ó Súileabháin or Ó Súilleabháin eventually became O'Sullivan, and later Sullivan. O' in front of the Irish surname means *grandson*. The surname, Sullivan, roughly translated, means "hawk-eyed." Most Sullivans dropped the O' when they migrated to America.

After the Norman Invasion in 1066 A.D., the Sullivans drifted to various Irish Counties, Cork and Kerry among them. This migration was followed by centuries of conflict against the Normans and, eventually, the English. The history of the warrior Sullivans is replete with stories of great victories and even greater defeats.

The Sullivans

The saga of Six Moquette Row took root in 1840 when John Sullivan married Mary Driscoll in County Cork, Ireland. Irish genealogical studies are somewhat limited for this period because many records were destroyed in fires and other catastrophes. John's birth and death dates are unknown. Mary Driscoll was born in 1808 and died in 1894.

On January 15, 1843, their son, Denis, was born in County Cork, Ireland. He married Ellen Cronin in Ireland in the late 1850's. Very little is known of their early life. Sometime during 1863 Denis traveled to Liverpool, England, and booked passage to sail to America. His immigration processing took place at Castle Garden, NY, where he initially settled into one of the Irish communities in lower New York City.

Denis worked at a number of unspecified jobs, eventually working as a "hatter" at the Waring Hat Company, in Yonkers, NY. By 1868, he had moved to Orchard Street in Yonkers, NY, but later settled his family at 8 1/2 Lafayette Street, Yonkers, where Ellen and their three children, John, James, and Mary, joined him. Their fourth child, Catherine, was born on September 25, 1869. Regrettably, Ellen died in childbirth.

Concurrently, around 1840 in County Mayo, Ireland, Patrick Duffy married Mary Cunningham. Little is known of the Duffys other than the fact that their daughter, Sarah Duffy, was born in County Mayo on May 30, 1850. Eventually, Sarah immigrated to America prior to 1869, where she met and married Denis Sullivan on November 10, 1870. They married a little over a year after Denis's first wife, Ellen's, death. Together, Denis and Sarah had nine (9) children, bringing Denis's total number of children to thirteen (13). The third of Sarah's children (and Denis's seventh) was Patrick Sullivan (April 3, 1876 – August 13, 1911), whose lineage is followed in this story.

Although it would be constructive in interpreting family history, it is difficult to arrive at a definitive description of Denis as a husband or parent. Clearly what is known, thus far, is not flattering. He was considered to be a staunch disciplinarian, who often used punitive actions to bring about the behavior he desired of his children. Exile to coal bins, dark closets, and whippings appear to be part of his repertoire. There is little evidence that he was either loving or compassionate. He clearly evolved from the "children should be seen and not heard" school of parenting.

In the late 1890's his son, Patrick Sullivan, met and fell in love with Mary Carroll. This relationship did not bode well with Denis, who vehemently opposed their plan to marry. As a laborer, Denis accumulated enough money to purchase a home in a middle-class neighborhood at 8 ½ Lafayette Street in the central city of Yonkers, NY. Mary Carroll did not fit his plans for his son. Her family was not as fortunate and lived in a rented row house, owned by the Alexander Smith Carpet Co., in an area of North Yonkers generally referred to as poverty row. Denis felt that his son, Patrick, was marrying beneath his social class. When Patrick and Mary did wed on May 17, 1899, Denis disowned his son. On their wedding day none of the Sullivans attended the wedding and the shades in their family home were drawn, signifying a death in the family. Denis Sullivan was unforgiving.

When on August 13, 1911, Patrick died unexpectedly at age 35, he left his wife destitute with five children, the oldest being eleven (twin boys – Joseph and Vincent), and the youngest (Patrick Arthur) born eighteen days (18) after his father's death. Despite the desperate circumstances that his daughter-in-law and five grandchildren were in, Denis did nothing to comfort or support his grief- stricken and impoverished family. This lack of compassion was a point of contention between the Carrolls and Sullivans that severely strained inter-family relationships. Family folklore has it that when Mary Oates Carroll (Nana), the mother of Patrick's wife, Mary (Mom), died on January 25, 1923, her dying words were to condemn Denis and Sarah Sullivan. The Sullivan children were resentful of their Sullivan grandparents, having limited contact with them throughout their life.

The Carrolls

In the early 1810's, James Oates (surname later changed by immigration officials to Otis) married Sarah Reynolds in Elfin, Ireland. Their daughter, Mary Otis (later referred to as Nana), was born in County Cavan, Ireland, on August 6, 1836. In 1864, she married Bernard Carroll, who was born in County Roscommon, Ireland, on January 12, 1839. They were married in Beacon, NY. Together Bernard and Mary (Nana) parented seven children, the last of which was Mary (Mom), who was born on June 26, 1877. Mary (Mom) became the widow of Patrick Sullivan.

Although little is known of the Sullivans during this period, a great deal is known of the Carrolls. Bernard arrived in America from Ireland somewhere between 1859 and 1861. Upon arriving in America, he migrated west and on April 20, 1861 he enlisted as a private in the Union Army's 14th Indiana Volunteer Regiment Co. F. His disability discharge papers (Intestinal disease - February 16, 1863) states that he was 5'7" tall with a light complexion, blue eyes, and brown hair. His prior occupation was listed as a farmer. He was considered to be a loving father and a good provider. Bernard died in Yonkers, NY, on July 8, 1884

If limited to one-word descriptions, one would say that Bernard was adventurous, and Mary (Nana) was feisty. They are remembered as being a loving, generous, and endearing couple, who faced adversity with faith based in traditional Catholicism and the strength that brought their family, and later the Sullivan children, safely thru many difficult times. Mary (Nana) died in Yonkers, NY on January, 1923

Like their parents, the seven Carroll children were kind and caring; the extent of their generosity is described throughout this story. In 1911, Nana Carroll and her sons, John and Barney, saved Mary (Mom) and her five children from a life of hardship by taking them into their home at Six Moquette Row, Yonkers, NY. There they were sheltered and cared for until they reached adulthood and married, or, in Vincent's case, died in a work-related accident. Mary (Mom) lived at Six Moquette Row until her death on April 25, 1952 at age seventy-four. She never remarried after her husband Patrick died on August 13, 1911.

Mary (Nana) lived a healthy life until an accidental fall hastened her demise at age 86. She was the matriarch of her family whose intelligence and sense of humor helped them overcome overwhelming difficulties. Nana Carroll had a quick wit, a fiery temper, and deep religious conviction. Small in frame, her generosity was limitless. Her life was devoted to caring for her children, especially her sons, John and Barney, daughter, Mary (Mom), and her five grandchildren, all of whom lived with her at Six Moquette (Poverty) Row. When necessary, she worked as a housekeeper but saw her primary responsibility as caring for her family. Although she remained the grandmother, her sons, John and Barney became the father figures for the Sullivan children. They financially supported whoever resided at Moquette Row.

What follows is the remarkable story of Six Moquette Row.

Acknowledgments

Six Moquette Row represents the collective efforts of many to preserve the memory of the Sullivan/Carroll families; two families united by the marriage of Patrick Sullivan and Mary (Mom) Carroll on May 17, 1899, and *blended* into one household after the devastatingly tragic death of Patrick on August 13, 1911.

Roland Sullivan and Sr. Gloria Sullivan, O.S.U., (grandchildren of Mary [Mom] Carroll Sullivan) graciously provided extensive documentation and shared childhood memories that facilitated the reconstruction of social and historical events of this time. Their desire to memorialize the blended family was the driving force behind this book's completion. Grandchildren, Janice Sullivan, Mary Sullivan Flinn, Joseph Baldwin and John Sullivan, Jr., as well as great-grandson John Sullivan, III, researched information that helped piece together significant events of the past. As a result, future generations of the Sullivan/Carroll bloodline will learn of and appreciate the extraordinary history and sacrifices of their ancestors.

Beyond the contributions of Roland and Gloria Sullivan, Six Moquette Row would not have been completed without the active participation of grandson, Joseph Baldwin. Joe was the last member of the Mary Carroll/Patrick Sullivan bloodline to live at Six Moquette Row, moving out in 1952 after the death of Mom Sullivan. His incredible memory of Yonkers and Moquette Row and exceptional editorial skills were indispensable.

The contributions of granddaughters, Janice Sullivan and Mary Sullivan Flinn, are acknowledged and appreciated. Their input helped frame a picture of the blended family and the challenges they faced between 1911 and 1985.

Research engines, such as Ancestry.com, History.com, and Wikipedia were excellent tools in reconstructing the history of Yonkers, NY, and the various components that made it a vibrant city. These resources, along with the assistance of the Yonkers Historical Society and Yonkers Reference Librarian, John Favareau (Yonkers Riverfront Library), helped make this overwhelming tasks a very manageable one. Likewise, the clerical staff of the Records Division at Yonkers City Hall was generous with their time and knowledge, processing many documents immediately upon request.

Always available to assist in the area of family genealogy was Donald Flinn (husband to Mary Sullivan Flinn). Frequently, he provided needed information by uncovering and certifying many historical facts.

Editing text is a daunting task and always a thankless one. The unselfish contributions of Theresa Sullivan, Eileen Lange (The Comma Nazi), Joseph Baldwin, and Gloria Sullivan, in this regard, cannot be undervalued. Their determination to achieve editorial excellence is clearly reflected in the end product that follows. Marianne Baldwin is acknowledged for her work on designing the Blended Family Tree Chart.

Thanks to realtor and friend, Sheila Clarke, for arranging for the authors to visit one of the remaining Moquette Row units. This visit helped to refresh old memories and frame the setting of this story.

Newly discovered distant relatives, Patricia Carney, Joan Carney, and Maureen O'Clair helped fill in gaps in family history that were previously unknown to the grandchildren. Through them, a greater knowledge of great-grandparents, Denis and Sarah Sullivan (parents of Patrick Sullivan), was acquired. Calie Patterson's technical assistance to Sr. Gloria Sullivan, O.S.U., was greatly appreciated. Historian and Yonkersonian, Robert Faigle, was extremely helpful in reconstructing the history of Yonkers as it impacted the blended family. Trish Faigle's (his wife) consistent encouragement insured that this book remained focused and on task.

To all who participated in the writing of this book, the grandchildren of the blended family are forever grateful. The story of this strong, determined family need not end here. Thus, it is the charge of future generations to continue the saga of the Sullivan/Carroll bloodline.

Prologue

Lancaster, PA is a historical treasure of great sociological significance. This small city situated in the southern central part of Pennsylvania attracts thousands of tourists each year; not because of its natural scenic beauty or its favorable geographic position. The primary attraction in Lancaster is a Christian sect of Americans known as the Amish People, more commonly referred to as The Pennsylvania Dutch.

Although interesting from a historical perspective, the national curiosity about the Amish is not their deeply rooted religious convictions. It is their lifestyle that is so apparent in the practice of those religious beliefs. It is in the way they have chosen to live their lives. The Amish have frozen in time a period in our country's evolution that preceded the discoveries and inventions of the nineteenth and twentieth century.

If one wanted to know how their ancestors lived a little more than a century ago, a visit to Lancaster is a perfect starting point. The Amish refuse to adopt modern technology, choosing instead, to live a very simple lifestyle. They live without the benefits of electricity, automobiles, radios, televisions, computers, the internet, and other modern devices. They believe strongly in the family unit and adhere to strict family practices and customs.

Fidelity and loyalty to family is of primary importance to them. For instance, when children have a financial or social need, it is the family that addresses that need. The Amish do not depend upon or welcome governmental intervention. In fact, they rally against it. Care of the elderly is also of primary importance. In their twilight years, the elderly are not sent to nursing homes to live out the remaining years. They are cared for by family at home. This is seldom the case in contemporary society. Their lifestyle is analogous to that which existed in America in the early 1900's.

Between 1890 and 1925, the world was catapulted into a new and unfamiliar way of life. Inventions, which at one time taxed the limits of man's imagination, were being introduced at a startling rate. Although spearheaded by American inventors, like Henry Ford and Thomas Edison, new wonders bombarded humanity from every corner of the globe. Most of the world enthusiastically embraced these changes; the Amish rejected them.

For a generation raised on smartphones, Facebook and the internet it is difficult to conceptualize that man lived *once upon a time* without indoor plumbing, paved streets, cars, jet planes, radios, televisions, cell phones, computers, and all of the conveniences of today's technological society. In a span of only thirty years (1895-1925), modern technology changed the world in which we live.

The collective genius of that period is reflected in the lifestyle of today. The grandparents and great-grandparents of today's children lived through and participated in the greatest transition civilization has ever witnessed. Contemporary society is the end product of that transition. Lancaster, PA, is representative of the world that was left behind.

Today people focus on the present and future with limited interest in the past. And lacking sensitivity for the contributions of past generations, the existing way of life is often taken for granted. There is a great interest in future generations, but little regard for those who preceded us; those to whom we should be eternally grateful, namely, our ancestors.

However, our insensitivity to our past is not completely our fault. Our ancestors did not leave blueprints on how to reconstruct their lives. To do so, genealogists must recreate the past, much like one tries to reassemble a very complicated jigsaw puzzle that has thousands of little pieces that seem to fit together. It is only through analyzing tombstones, studying salvaged letters, researching old newspapers and legal documents, such as birth, death, marriage, and baptismal certificates that the mysteries of the past begin to unravel.

Despite exhaustive research, the larger portion of family historical information is gleaned through folklore, i.e., stories of life gone by that have been passed down from generation to generation. Unfortunately, over time, like most word of mouth chronicles, it becomes more difficult to differentiate fact from fiction. Thus, reconstructing the lives of those who have gone before us is a daunting task. Quite often it is an invention built upon a truthful basis. People are oblivious to the pain and sacrifice that enabled us to become who we are. When we speak of our predecessors, we speak in factual, as opposed to emotional terms with little regard as to who they were and what they were like.

When it comes to the past, our highly organized society attempts to bundle humanity into neat little labeled packages that can be placed in larger containers and stored on those proverbial shelves called family trees. Even the vocabulary that we use to describe our ancestors is unemotional; therefore, we think of them in the same cold terms. The word *ancestor* is almost as antiseptic as *forebear*. Both words are as devoid of emotion as are *forerunner, predecessor,* or, God forbid, *antecedent.*

These terms don't speak of love or hate, or suffering and pain, or even of goodness or evil. They simply place our DNA into a very neat cubicle. But is that all our ancestors are? Are we just as devoid of feeling as a tree leaf that is hung lower than great grandmother Sarah's branch or on higher limb than Auntie Mildred; whereas Uncle Phillip is parallel, and God knows where little Billy's container goes. But shouldn't it be much more than that? Is this all they are to us or what we will be to future generations?

There is a symbiotic relationship connecting the past with the present and the present with the future; a connection that has life and feelings. It isn't devoid of human emotions, or just a marker on a diagram or genealogical chart. In order to understand and respect our predecessors, we must first know them. And knowing them is what the story of Six Moquette Row attempts to do: introduce us to the blended family from whence we came.

.   .   .   .   .   .

The blended family of this story was much more than a dot on a chart. It was a living, feeling, and caring entity. The members were active and loving human beings who had great affection for one another. They would never have survived if this were not the case.

Uncles John and Barney Carroll were two single men who could have had a great deal of material comfort for themselves, but chose to open their home and share what little they had with their parent, siblings, nephews and a niece. Accurately preserving their story preserves their memory, as well as that of the Sullivan children, their mother and grandmother. Preserving family memories is synonymous with preserving a family's history.

Most of the details of The Carroll/Sullivan blended family have originated from three of the original five Sullivan children - Joseph, John, and Mary. The remaining two children, Arthur (Patrick) and Vincent died at relatively young ages, prior to the time when this information was collected.

Factual information has been gleaned from a variety of validated sources, including legal documents, newspapers, and anecdotal recollections. Memories of the three aforementioned Sullivan children filled in the gaps. An analysis of both created an accurate image of real people facing and conquering real problems in a very difficult environment. The irrefutable facts are that our ancestors were common people who behaved in a very courageous way.

In all likelihood, if the Carroll brothers did not rescue (or, in contemporary terms, take in) the Sullivan children in 1911, they would have been split up and placed in foster homes without the benefit of family or siblings with whom to interact. This was, after all, a common practice of the day and had happened to some of the other grandchildren of the Denis Sullivan. Fortunately for the children of Patrick Sullivan, this was not the case. The five Sullivan children (Joseph, Vincent, John, Mary, and Arthur {Patrick}), were rescued from poverty by John and Barney Carroll (brothers of Mary Carroll Sullivan), who raised them as their own. The children were not rescued by the Denis Sullivans of the world, who were more than capable of doing so. And therein is the story of unselfish and unconditional love.

The authors hope to humanize the ancestral tree of the Bernard Carroll/ Denis Sullivan blood line. The direct descendants of Bernard Carroll and Denis Sullivan have died long ago as have their siblings and children. What remains are six devoted grandchildren who hope to preserve the memory of this family's bloodline with the most-accurate information available at the time of this writing.

This story is far from complete. Nonetheless, it is a story that should be told. It is a story of a family whose loyalty and devotion to one another enabled them to overcome very difficult obstacles. Together, they survived in a very harsh world. The trials and tribulations they faced are contained within the storyline. Hopefully, the personalities of the participants are also reflected in these pages. The love they experienced and the pain they suffered will be remembered in the hearts of those who follow.

With brief reference to the period prior to 1894, this story begins with the marriage of Mary Jane Carroll to Patrick Sullivan on May 17, 1899. Both Mary and Patrick's parents were Irish immigrants who came to America to seek a more promising future. Unfortunately, prejudices having to do with an artificial class structure resulted in the rejection of Mary Carroll by Denis and Sarah Sullivan (Patrick's parents). This rejection subsequently led to further rejection of the five grandchildren who were the product of this marriage, even after tragedy struck; the tragedy being the untimely death of Patrick Sullivan on August 13, 1911.

The lives of the Sullivan children were played out in a row house in North Yonkers. Six Moquette Row wasn't a palace, but it was their castle and remained so for sixty plus years. This is the story of the family that occupied Six Moquette Row between July, 1886, and April, 1952. It is a story of their successes and failures, the happiness they shared and the suffering they endured. It is a story that reflects the greatness of this country, as mirrored in the greatness of its people.

Introduction

Externally, Six Moquette Row could not be distinguished from its neighbors. They were all small brick "row" homes with two stories, ample backyards, and front stoops, which were used for friendly banter, supervision of the many children who called the row houses their homes, and getting a "breath of fresh air."

There the resemblances ended. Each family established a unique spirit. Inside the walls of Number Six that spirit was one of *acceptance, cooperation, shared laughter and remarkable mutual love and support.* Initially, this spirit was established by a young Irish couple, Bernard and Mary Carroll, who had moved to Yonkers from Beacon, New York, and found employment and companionship with other Irish émigrés, and a home of their own!

As the years passed, the spirit never dimmed. Generation succeeded generation. Normally, there were three generations (sometimes four) enjoying life together at Six Moquette Row. Mary (Nana) Carroll and Bernard (Pop) Carroll were succeeded by their daughter, Mary Jane, who married Patrick Sullivan. However, she was widowed after twelve years of marriage and left with five children. Mary Jane Carroll became Mary (Mom) Sullivan and endeared herself to her children and grandchildren.

What of the spirit that had enlivened Six Moquette Row? It has not lost any of its luster. The spirit of Mary and Bernard Carroll lives on, no longer at Six Moquette Row but wherever their great-grandchildren and subsequent generations gather to share in *acceptance, cooperation, laughter, mutual love and support.*

Inspiration comes in many forms. It may assume the guise of a much-loved poem from childhood or a prayer that is always available. At times, it resides in well-matched companions or a group of friends. It is an improvised sibling who has not found friendship among family members or in the joy of sharing music, conversations, or games with others.

A generation of Sullivan children has been inspired by their grandmother, known to all as Mom Sullivan. Mom was not blessed by luxury or, even, moderate wealth. Her life was austere but happy, in spite of the early death of her husband Patrick, and later, the deaths of three of her five grown children, Vincent, Arthur, and Mary. She did not take refuge in sorrow. Instead, she projected energy, satisfaction, and love for her family and friends.

Mom dressed her age. Until the end, she wore a housedress and her long gray hair in a bun, as she did in her youth, regardless of the changing styles of the time. She was young with the young and grew up with her grandchildren as they matured. She was their companion and willingly joined in their childhood games that changed as they grew older. They loved visiting and spending time with her.

Mom's home at Six Moquette Row was filled with the songs of her canaries, the antics of her obviously intelligent dog, Fox, and her parrot, Polly, with its ever expanding vocabulary. Polly would help her rouse her youngest son, Arthur, by loudly mimicking her voice. He would call out "come in" when the doorbell rang, and give an impressive and faithful boost to the call of passing fire engines. He would also join in with the neighbors' efforts to call their children back home.

One of the greatest pleasures of childhood was to enjoy a meal at Mom's. Her unrivaled gravy, vegetables, meats and breads were followed by her delicious apple pie (which was uniquely unsweetened so everyone could sweeten their own piece). During and after the meal the talk, laughter and friendly kibitzing added the final touches to a wonderful repast.

This then is it. Of course, one could add much more or even write less. But, this is the interpretation by one of those fortunate grandchildren for whom one of life's inspirations was Mary Jane Carroll Sullivan, - "Mom."

Sr. Gloria Sullivan, O.S.U.

Chapter 1

The Rescue

✦

During the international trade wars of the early 1600's, the Dutch West India Company (WIC), a private conglomerate of Dutch merchants, was chartered by the Dutch National Assembly to conduct economic warfare against Spain and Portugal. The WIC established fiefdoms (patroonships) to govern various regions of North America. One of the patroonships was The New Netherlands Company, which managed the areas of New York, Connecticut, New Jersey and Delaware. Under the supervisory umbrella of the greatly mismanaged WIC, the mission of The New Netherlands Company was to exploit the fur trade industry in North America.

In 1645, the director of The New Amsterdam Company was Willem Kieft. Kieft granted a 24,000 acre tract of land to Andriaen van Donck. This parcel became known as Yonkers, NY.

Van Donck's intent was that Yonkers would serve the environmental needs of a small farming and logging community. But its prime location on the Hudson River was ideally suited for it to become much more. Within two hundred years the shift from agrarian to manufacturing was well underway. From its waterfront, goods were shipped north to Albany, NY, and south to New York City, the Atlantic Ocean and beyond. Yonkers was ideally positioned to accommodate the demands of the industrial revolution that would soon follow.

In the late nineteenth century, Broadway (also called U.S. 9 or The Albany Post Road) was the primary roadway joining New York City and Albany, NY, a distance of approximately 150 miles. Broadway's north/south nine-mile passageway through Yonkers provided an easy and efficient division of the city into two major sections, west Yonkers and east Yonkers. The city was further divided into north and south with its line of demarcation at Getty

Square, which was the heart of the rapidly growing industrial center. Getty Square was 18 miles from Wall Street, New York City.

The City of Hills and The Terrace City (nicknames used to reference Yonkers) more than lived up to its appellation. Its landscape was often compared to Rome or San Francisco. Its many hills rose from sea level to more than four hundred feet. Traversing the hills of Yonkers was always a daunting task, especially for those whose primary source of transportation was either by foot or bicycle. Fall and winter snows were particularly perilous. Narrow, unpaved, and, often, cluttered streets were the rule in most areas east of North Broadway, especially in those sections where the poor resided. But prevailing economic conditions were such that many unfortunate Yonkersonians did not have a choice. They were forced to live in crowded and sub-standard neighborhoods that contemporary standards would classify as slums.

Coinciding with its geographic division, life on the westside of North Broadway was very different from that of the east. Many luxurious homes and Victorian mansions with panoramic views of the Hudson River peppered the western countryside. For the most part, those homes were inhabited by the rich and very rich who lived in this suburban community close to the center of New York City. While people east of Broadway languished, those on the west flourished. This dichotomy of wealth created a class division that clearly delineated the boundaries for the indigent. This partitioning by wealth simultaneously cultivated a ghetto mentality that was a prescription for crime and violence.

The cause of this chasm in class structure fell indisputably at the doorstep of rapid and uncontrolled population growth. In 1865, at the end of the Civil War, the population of Yonkers was less than 18,000. However, by the turn of the century it had exceeded 48,000, and by 1910, the number soared to more than 80,000. This population surge coincided with the industrialization of Yonkers and analogous with its rapid growth; Yonkers became a city in 1872. Its strategic location on the Hudson River dictated that its transformation from an agrarian community to an industrial complex was inevitable. The construction of the Otis Elevator Company along the Hudson River in the 1850's, as well as that of the Alexander Smith & Sons Carpet Company (North Yonkers) in 1865, made Yonkers a magnet for Americans and immigrants seeking employment and a new life.

The Shop or The Carpet Shop (as it was called by the Yonkersonians) alone employed more than 4,000 workers. In 1862, the Waring Hat Company, the largest in the nation, joined many other businesses that established its corporate headquarters in the City of Hills.

Unfortunately, this stream of laborers brought with it all of the problems of a rapidly growing society that was ill prepared for a large population influx. As a result, the social unbalance put the city in turmoil. Narrow roads that were originally constructed for horse, pedestrian, and bicycle traffic became shared spaces with automobiles, delivery wagons, horse drawn trolleys and carriages, sanitation wagons and the like. In the evening pedestrians, bicycles, and horse- drawn trolleys joined the fracas.

Often the pressures of collectively forcing such diverse components into occupying the same inadequate space manifested itself in contentious behavior and violence. Chaos and crime ruled the streets as issues of *right of way* were frequently adjudicated by violence, as opposed to negotiation.

Compounding this problem, raw garbage, human waste, litter and horse-droppings accumulated for days on end, significantly impacted the horrendous living conditions that were already unsanitary. Quite often the city noise was deafening, and street odors were putrid. For the city fathers, the problems were insurmountable.

The area east of North Broadway was flooded with homeless transients seeking both shelter and work. West of Broadway, the "bosses" lived in opulence. Those very same bosses controlled city government. Thus, the wealthy constructed their giant fiefdoms on the backs of the poor. They redirected problems from their lavish neighborhoods to those of the less fortunate. The wealthy seemed to be oblivious of the conflicts that took place beyond their little enclave.

An increase in crime, especially robberies and assaults, was rendering the streets unsafe and, as reported in the newspapers of the day, "roughs and rowdies were taking over the town." The constables (usually rented from New York City), who were employed to control crime, were considered to be ineffective tools of politicians. A permanent solution had to be found.

The first Yonkers Police Department was established on March 30, 1871. Unruly streets were soon patrolled by foot and mounted police, as well as horse-drawn police wagons. Quite often their presence only added to the madness. The first Yonkers Fire Department was established in 1896. Yonkers was evolving almost as quickly as its population spurt into an independent entity. Although the goal of the City Council was to insure the safety of the entire city, the bulk of protection went to the wealthier neighborhoods west of North Broadway.

.   .   .   .   .   .

John and Barney Carroll were brothers who, along with their mother Mary, lived on the eastside of Broadway at Six Moquette Row. They rented their *row house* from the Alexander Smith Carpet Company, more commonly referred to as The Shop, where they were employed as hourly workers. On the morning of November 13, 1911, they made a decision that would permanently change their lives and the lives of their sister, Mary, and her five children. On that day, they became heroes.

Monday, November 13, 1911, was a bitter cold night with temperatures plummeting below twenty degrees. Periodic snow swirls and wind gusts exceeding 28 miles an hour impeded trolley, horse, and foot traffic, eventually bringing them to a halt. The absence of traffic meant the absence of noise and conflict, normally a welcomed relief for the poorer neighborhoods. And although the wind-chill was life threatening, it did help replace the dank odors of the ghetto with fresh and vibrant air. It was a mixed blessing.

The silence of the night was ominous. John and Barney had an eerie feeling when at 6 p.m.; they began their two-mile up-hill walk from their home at Six Moquette Row to their sister, Mary's, cold-water flat at 74 St. Joseph's Avenue.

The chill factor was worse than the brothers had anticipated. The damp air that settled between the Hudson River and the Long Island Sound seeped through their outer clothing, completely soaking them. The cold was almost unbearable. The three-day freeze had not shown any signs of letting up and the sub-freezing temperatures made survival perilous for the poor. Haze from a late afternoon rain caused moments of zero visibility. The dim flames from the recently lighted gas street lamps were virtually useless in this fall storm. Those who were unfortunate enough to be outside would be chilled to the bone. But the brothers had to keep walking. They were on a mission that could not be delayed any longer.

This early evening trek was much more difficult than the brothers had expected. The walk was steep and arduous. But they had spoken enough about their sister's predicament; their minds were made up. This time, they would not take "no" for an answer. Their sister, Mary, was coming home, and one way or another, they were not returning without her and her five children.

The Carroll brothers were the gentle giants of North Yonkers. Everyone respected their kindness and good-natured personalities. They were jovial but reserved. Above all, they were gentlemen. They both had that rugged reddish complexion and the quiet Irishman's demeanor that cautioned all that beneath their velvet gloves were fists of steel. For that reason alone, no one ever attempted to take advantage of their generosity.

The Carrolls lived in the row houses directly across the street from the Alexander Smith Carpet Company on Nepperhan Avenue in North Yonkers. This location was ideal for the brothers, considering the long hours they each worked at The Shop to earn a meager salary of less than seven hundred dollars a year.

Together, they were the caregivers and sole supporters for their mother, Mary Oates Carroll, more commonly called "Nana." Nana was in excellent health considering her seventy-two years of stressful living. Migrating from Ireland in 1851 had taken its toll on her and her family. When they entered the United States, their family surname was changed to Otis by the immigration authorities.

Nana was tiny, not quite five feet tall, thin, weighting about ninety-five pounds, and growing fragile. But even so, she was *sharp as a tack* and as *spunky* as a teenager. Only recently did she need help from her sons to ascend and descend the stairs to her bedroom on the second floor of their tiny home. She would pass the day on the first floor, sitting in her stuffed chair by the living room window. Other than requiring assistance to navigate the steep staircase, she maintained herself and her independence. Like her children, she was "good- natured and fun loving." She was known to possess the quickest wit in the family, even in her advanced years. She loved to cook and took the responsibility of maintaining her sons' ample girth seriously.

Her son John, at forty-six years old, had been working at *The Shop* since he was thirteen. He was a massive young man with a large barreled chest, thick neck and muscular arms. He was barely six feet tall, but his large body made him appear much taller. He was 215 lbs of solid muscle. He was recently widowed; it was a childless marriage. After his wife's death in 1909, he returned home to live with his mother, and brother (Barney).

John had rugged good looks and broad shoulders. His piercing hazel eyes were his most-striking feature. Despite being American born, he had acquired a bit of his mother's Irish brogue. Of the two brothers, John was clearly the more jovial. He had a zest for life that was infectious, and his generosity frequently exceeded his meager wages. He loved children and animals. The parrot, dog, and duck that lived with them in their six-room row house were the product of John's big heart and his successful animal rescue attempts. His once red hair had thinned significantly. What remained had already turned gray.

Barney was thirty-five years old and a youthful carbon copy of his older brother. He was about an inch shorter and twenty pounds heavier. Like John, he also began his working career at the carpet shop when he turned fourteen. He was as muscular as John but, unlike his brother, maintained a full head of auburn hair. He too had the piercing family hazel eyes. He tended to be more pensive and more serious than John. But, as always, he yielded to his older brother's age and wisdom. They never disagreed and always thought and acted as one. Barney dated from time to time but seemed to avoid serious female relationships. He loved children and thought of having a family, but that was always in the distant future. But tonight he would come face to face with his distant future.

Their jobs at the Alexander Smith Carpet Company required strength and agility. They worked long and demanding hours. Overtime had taken its toll, and they both were beginning to feel their level of energy diminishing. Nonetheless, they regularly worked beyond their fifty-five hour work week, especially since their sister, Mary's husband, Patrick, had died. Their combined income, meager as it was, helped to provide for their mother, sister and her children. If nothing else, the Carrolls stuck together.

As the brothers forged forward to their sister, Mary's, cold-water flat they did not speak to one another. For one thing, it was too cold to talk. For another, there was nothing more to say. They had made their decision.

Their sister, Mary Carroll Sullivan, was a slight, determined thirty-four-year old woman who had faced more than her fair share of personal tragedies. But she faced them with dignity, never complaining, and never asking for help. Anyone who met her would quickly discover that showing sympathy for her would be a big mistake. She was never one to feel sorry for herself, nor to tolerate anyone who felt sorry for her. Her recent difficulties were no exception. Offering Mary charity was out of the question and potentially life threatening.

Their parents, Mary (Nana) Otis and Bernard Carroll, Sr., were married in Fishkill, New York, in 1864. Daughter, Mary, and sons, John, and Bernard (called Barney) were three of the six children born to them. Barney, Sr., was an Irish immigrant and disabled Civil War veteran who required extensive care. Their daughter, Mary, was seventeen years old when he died in 1894. The family resources were limited, and the Carrolls were poor. After Barney, Sr's, death, the children were forced to forgo a formal education after the fourth grade to work at The Shop.

Like her brothers, Mary possessed a pleasant disposition and a kind heart. John and Barney paid particular attention to their "baby sister." (This appellation that was fostered upon her at birth remained into her adult life). She was shorter than John, and Barney. At age 34, her angelic face was beginning to show signs of the trials and tribulations she had been forced to endure. She, like her mother, Nana, lacked height but had acquired her brothers' girth. Her rosy complexion, graying hair, and hazel eyes projected an air of calm and confidence that often masked her inner fears. As her family grew, people began to call her "Mom." When she didn't respond to being "Baby Mary," "Mom" became her unofficial forename for the rest of her life.

Like her brothers, Mary's independent streak and her enormous personal strength kept her positive and focused. A weaker person would have turned bitter and resentful. Her husband's (Patrick Sullivan) unexpected death on August 13, 1911, marked the lowest point in her short life. This horrific tragedy brought her to her knees. She had four children and was nine months pregnant with her fifth child at that time. Her deplorable living conditions after her child's birth (Patrick Arthur Sullivan) were the reasons for John and Barney's unannounced visit on that cold November night. Her brothers were determined to intervene. Their "baby sister" needed help, and they were there to give it, even if it was against her will.

·   ·   ·   ·   ·   ·

Mary (Mom) had married her soul-mate, Patrick Sullivan, after a very short courtship. Patrick was a year younger than Mary and, like her brothers, was the consummate gentleman. He was strong, athletic, and exceedingly handsome. His slim six foot frame was that of the perfect athlete and his rating as the finest semi-professional baseball pitcher in the city of Yonkers gave him recognition wherever he went. His hazel eyes and red hair made him easily identifiable. His friends called him *Rusty*.

Rusty was smitten by Mary Carroll. From the first moment, he laid eyes on her he was determined to make her his wife. But, his determination was not shared by his affluent family who had expected him to marry someone of greater wealth and social stature. His parents, Denis and Sarah Duffy Sullivan, aspired to be part of the *West of Broadway* crowd. They not only discouraged their son from marrying Mary Carroll, they forbade it. When the couple did wed, the Sullivans refused to attend his wedding and disowned him. The marriage, which took place on May 17, 1899, at St. Joseph's Roman Catholic

Church on Ashburton Avenue in Yonkers, was not attended by any member of the Sullivan family. On that day, the Sullivans wore black armbands and pulled the shades down in the windows of their home, signifying that they were in mourning. Their displeasure with their son's marriage was made known to all. The newlyweds started their married life without the blessing or support of the affluent Sullivan clan. But choosing Mary was a decision that Patrick never regretted.

As the family provider, Patrick reduced his commitment to baseball and worked as a butcher in the Yonkers Meat Market. In 1907, he became a professional firefighter in the Yonkers Fire Department. Patrick and Mary quickly gained respect and stature in Yonkers social settings, and they became active community members. They were popular and independent.

In the tradition of a typical Irish Catholic family of the time, children came quickly to them. The first to arrive in 1900 were twin brothers, Joseph and Vincent. Five years later son, John (1905) was born, followed in 1909 by daughter, Mary. They doted over their children and were a model family. Patrick was respected for his strength in not yielding to his parents' prejudices. He was loved and admired by his brother-in-laws, John and Barney, and adored by Nana Carroll. This new Sullivan family was in a good place.

However, good health was not in Patrick's destiny. In 1909, he contracted tuberculosis and spent more than a year in Raybrook Hospital (Raybrook, NY), a facility fifty miles from his pregnant wife and four children. Unfortunately, on August 13, 1911 while being treated for tuberculosis, he died in surgery from peritonitis, the result of a ruptured appendix. His son, Patrick (Arthur), was born on August 29, 1911, sixteen days after Patrick's death.

At age thirty-four, Mary (Mom) Sullivan became a widow with five children without any significant source of income, the oldest children (Joseph and Vincent) being twin boys eleven years old and the youngest (Arthur) being a newborn. For all practical purposes, this Sullivan family was destitute and assistance from Patrick's family was not forthcoming. Even in death they did not accept the marriage of their son, Patrick, to Mary Carroll nor did they acknowledge their now five grandchildren. The risk of starvation or hypothermia to Mary and her children was very real; they were in trouble and time was running out.

·   ·   ·   ·   ·   ·

John and Barney were, at first, taken aback by the strong odor from the anthracite coal burning stoves that heated each of the six apartments that shared the space in this aged classical three-story wood structure at 74 St. Joseph's Avenue. But even the pungent smell of smoldering coal provided a welcomed relief from the cold outside. The gas-lit lamps in the narrow hallway cast an ominous glow as the brothers climbed the stairs to their sister's three-room flat on the top floor. As they approached the door to Mary's apartment, they braced themselves for what might well be the fight of their lives. As small as she was, Mary was every bit as intimidating as her brothers, and they believed her resistance would be formidable.

As the large right hand of John tapped on Mary's door, whispers and rustling could be heard from within the apartment. An unannounced evening visitor at any time in this North Yonkers neighborhood would be cause for concern, but on a stormy November night it was unfathomable. The silence that followed was frightening. After a few moments of inactivity, John rapped again. This time, his efforts elicited a very timid female response that inquired, "Who's there?"

"Mary...it's John and Barney," responded John, "it's ok, open up the door."

As Mary opened the door, the brothers were heartbroken by what they saw. Mary was fully clothed and wrapped in a tattered brown army blanket that hung loosely from her shoulders. She held her newborn son, Patrick Arthur, in her arms. In the background, wrapped in tattered blankets and huddled around a black pot-bellied coal stove, were her four other children. Clearly they were cold and terrified. Everyone was dressed in tattered winter clothing. The chilling cold within the apartment vaporized in the air as they spoke. If there were any doubts that the Carroll brothers had made the right decision, it was dispelled by what they saw.

When Joseph and Vincent saw their beloved and fun-loving uncles, their welcoming eyes lit up with recognition and joy. They rushed to embrace them. In eleven years of living, the twins had faced a lot of misfortune. Their father's untimely death, his wake that took place in this very apartment, and the fifty-man procession of Yonkers firemen that escorted their father's body to its interment in St. Joseph's Cemetery only a few months before were still fresh in their minds. They had expected their father to come home after being cured of tuberculosis. He had been away for a long time, but their anguish of separation was lessened by periodic visits to his bedside. His sudden death from an unanticipated illness deepened their grief.

They struggled to help their mother care for their younger brothers and sister, but their spirit was near broken. Instinctively, they knew they had to survive, and they worked at odd jobs, shared a newspaper route, and hoped to earn extra money shoveling snow when the storm finally abated. But underneath it all, their life's spirit was fast-leaving them.

Initially, it was difficult to tell Joseph and Vincent apart, but as the early years passed, it was clear that Joseph would be a little taller, and Vincent would be stockier. Following their father's death, Joseph assumed the role of a surrogate parent to his younger brother, John, while their sister, Mary, became Vincent's charge. Their newborn brother, Patrick, already being called Arthur, needed his mother's undivided attention, and she lovingly cared for him between working odd jobs and doing part-time shift work at The Shop. Arthur was her link to her deceased husband, a link that could only be broken by death.

The Sullivans struggled from hand-to-mouth on a daily basis for three months. Patrick's meager pension was not enough to sustain a growing family of five children. But Mary was fiercely independent and determined to survive in what was increasingly becoming a crueler world.

John, at age six, and Mary, at age three had difficulty understanding what was happening. They barely knew their father and longed to be like the other children in their neighborhood. They were always frightened, but they weren't quite sure what they were frightened about. Somehow they knew that when their uncles were around, things were going to be alright, and that made them feel safe.

"Good Lord, what has happened now?" Mary asked as she greeted her brothers who were now entering her flat.

"There's nothing wrong, Mary, we just came to talk to you," replied John.

"It's a horrible night outside, and bitter cold," replied Mary, as her stance became upright and rigid. The brothers knew all too well what that meant. Mary was resistant. "Enough of your stories, John. You must have a good reason to come here on a night like tonight, so what is it? Is this about Nana? Now sit, take off your wet coats and let me get you a warm cup of tea, and then let's hear it." John had already begun to crumble. But Barney stood firm.

"We won't be taking off our coats, and we won't be sitting, Mary, and we don't have time for tea," said Barney in a very stern voice. His eyes were fiery and penetrating as he stared at Mary until she finally looked away with a puzzled expression on her face. She wanted to demand answers on the spot, but she knew her brother, Barney, all too well. She could not push him around like she could John. He was not to be rushed. He would tell her the reason for their visit in due time, and not a moment sooner. So… she stood with her arms folded across her chest and waited; and, as moments passed in silence, her defenses softened.

Finally, as tears rolled down Barney's face, and as his eyes, that only a moment ago were spitting fire, began to show the gentle spirit behind his facade, he said, "Gather up your children and grab what belongings you can carry, and extinguish the kerosene lamps. We've come to take you home."

And that was that, no discussion, no argument. John gathered up the children; Barney collected all the items that Arthur would need, and Mary sat and wept. But unlike the tears she shed nightly for her deceased husband, her tears were of relief and joy. At the very darkest of times, and with Thanksgiving just weeks away, her brothers had given her the gift of hope. Despite her enormous grief, she felt relief.

Finally, when she composed herself and gathered that reservoir of strength that kept her strong, she pulled both brothers close and said, "What took you so long to get here; we have been sitting with our coats on all day waiting for you to come."

With a hardy laugh and a sigh of relief, John, replied, "We had to walk, the trolleys stopped running. And that's exactly how we are all going home."

.   .   .   .   .   .

John then began to organize the return trip. "Vincent, you're responsible for your sister, Mary. Joseph hold your brother, John's, hand and don't let him wander. Mary, wrap Arthur in a heavy blanket and keep him close to your body. It is going to be a cold, difficult walk."

He continued, this time speaking a little louder and quickly. His adrenaline was pumping, and he was anxious to get underway. His natural leadership skills had surfaced, and it was clear that he was in charge. Instinctively, everyone responded to his commands. "Barney, you and I will carry what we can and come back for the rest when the storm's over. I'll take the front; you take the back. Vincent, you and sister, Mary, line up behind me; Mary and Arthur, you're in the middle; and, Joseph and John, behind your mother. Remember, we must stick together, walk quickly, quietly, and do whatever Uncle Barney tells us to do. He is behind us and will be able to see better than I can."

And with that, this ragtag line of Carrolls and Sullivans began their journey into a new life.

As the procession lined up at the top St. Joseph's Avenue, Barney's primary concern was safety. With the increasing number of vagrants and unemployed wandering North Yonkers, this could be a very dangerous walk. Despite the diminishing winds, the wind-chill factor would be menacing. Barney calculated that the walk should take about a half hour, but any problems along the way could extend the journey and expose the children to even greater cold and, possibly, frostbite. In these troubled times, children and women were always easy targets for marauders who preyed upon the weak and vulnerable. Barney prayed that no one would be wandering the roads on a night as cold and foreboding as this. He and John did not encounter any problems on their trip to Mary's flat, and he was optimistic that the return trip to Moquette Row would be equally as safe and uneventful.

In reality, one look at John and Barney's massive size in their winter coats and their erect and determined walk would discourage any would-be assailant. The procession looked like five small trees sandwiched between two huge Redwoods. As they began their trek, Barney's eyes were focused on the path ahead. He would not allow anything to distract him. As they moved forward in unison, his eyes moved rapidly from side to side. Joseph, John, Vincent, and Mary huddled together in tight formation around Mary and Arthur. This clustering slowed their cadence but offered some protection from the periodic wind gusts that impeded vision.

Mary pulled Arthur close to her body, and his little face was barely visible beneath the blanket she had draped around her and his upper body. Unlike the apprehension that her brothers were feeling, Mary was surprisingly calm. For her, despite the elements, the worst was over. After months of loneliness and toil, she was returning to the security of her home and family. She knew she was doing what Patrick would have told her to do. She missed him desperately and had not had enough time to grieve or reminisce about the life they had shared or the dreams they were following. Perhaps now she could deal with those inner thoughts that she had bottled up within her. Now that there would be others to share in raising the children, she could take a few moments to deal with the realities of being a young widow. Maybe now she could be sad and not have to hide her sorrow. Regardless of how bad things were, they could only get better. She knew that she and her children would be safe.

Both Joseph and Vincent understood the meaning and the importance of the journey and took their responsibilities to guard their young charges seriously. In unison, they followed directions with their siblings in tow. They were strong, quiet young men who were managing to cope with the tragedy of a fatherless life. They loved their uncles and were excited about the prospect of living with them. Their uncles loved to joke and wrestle, and play ball, and do many of the things their friends' fathers did. It had been a longtime since their life was filled with laughter, and they knew that after they completed this difficult walk, laughter would return.

Little John and little Mary were cold and frightened. Uncle John told them to do what Joseph and Vincent told them to do, and so they did it. Vincent pulled Mary a little too hard at times, but she didn't complain. John walked a little faster than Joseph wanted because he was anxious to get to Nana Carroll's house. It seemed to him that his Uncle John was constantly asking if everyone was alright and Barney continued to reassure him that it was "all clear." Little John didn't know what that meant, but it made his uncles happy, and that was fine with him. Little did they know, then, that this walk would formulate a lifetime bond between Joseph and little John and Vincent and little Mary. For the younger two, their older twin brothers would forever be their confidants and protectors.

The procession walked a few steps to High Street, turned right and followed it to the end where it intersected with Ridge Avenue. Just before the High Street - Ridge Avenue intersection they encountered six men standing around a garbage can fire in a small field on the left side of the road. At first John did not see them, but as the mist cleared they were visible and only about twenty feet away. They were hard to see, but they were there. Barney shouted a gentle warning to John and the procession stopped. The brothers lowered the items they were carrying to the ground and freed up their hands and arms in the event that they had to defend themselves.

Simultaneously, one of the strangers noticed the procession and made an indecipherable comment to the remaining fire gatherers. The men turned and faced the travelers.

Before John could react, one to the men shouted, "Greetings travelers, come warm yourselves by our fire. What are you doing out on a night like tonight?"

"No thanks mate," replied Barney. "We've got to get these children out of the cold before they catch pneumonia. The little one is only two months old. We don't have far to go."

"Are you going down the stairway to Vineyard?" replied the stranger.

"Aye," said John, "and beyond that down to Orchard Street."

"Then hurry along mate, and if anyone stops you, tell them you're friends of Peter Finch and that anyone who interferes with you getting those children home will have to answer to him. Now move along and be careful. Take your belongings with you. We won't be needing them."

The brothers gathered up Mary's meager possessions, and they continued to the stairway that was fifty feet ahead of them. They slowly descended the narrow wooden stairway to Vineyard Avenue. This narrow passage protected them from the wind, but the darkness put John and Barney on even higher alert. Peter Finch's warning alerted them to the possibility of danger ahead. When they reached Vineyard Avenue, and just before they descended the final staircase that would take them to Orchard Street, Uncle John told them, "If anything happens along the way, run as fast as you can to Nana Carroll's house."

The warning frightened the children, but they were on their way again before they could think about it. They rushed across Vineyard Avenue and started down the final staircase, quickly arriving at Orchard Street. They were relieved to not have encountered any problems. The warmth of the stairwell had eased the pain of the bitter cold wind.

At Orchard Street, the procession turned left and walked 500 yards to Moquette Row, the first dead-end street on the right. They were almost home and no longer felt the cold air. Number 6 was on the right at the bottom of the hill. They could see its lights from where they were standing. Barney and John cautioned the children not to run, but their words fell on deaf ears. The children couldn't restrain themselves any longer. Off Joseph and Vincent ran, shouting and laughing with little John and Mary in tow.

Knocking on the door was not necessary. Nana Carroll had been seated in her chair by the front window from the time her sons left to retrieve Mary. She would not leave her post until they returned. When she heard the laughter and cheer of her grandchildren, she rushed to the door to welcome them. And even before she could close the front door, all four were telling her of the marvelous adventure they had just had. Their mother was right. The laughter was returning.

Mary (carrying Arthur), John, and Barney were a little slower at arriving at the door. They laughed as they watched the younger children run down the hill and greeted their grandmother. Their joy was only exceeded by that of Nana Carroll. The voices of the young had finally returned to Moquette

Row, and they were all safe. She reached out to take her youngest grandson from his mother's arms, an offer Mary readily accepted.

When the ragtag procession arrived, they were warmly greeted by an unnamed family parrot, duck, and Rex, the Fox Terrier. A very happy Nana Carroll was still being distracted by the younger four and it was anticipated that she would be busy for a long time. When she put her extended family to bed, she would finally have a chance to embrace her daughter, Mary.

Nana Carroll's hero sons stayed in the background and basked in the joy that had just entered their home. At least for the time being, their worries were over. It was after midnight when the Carrolls and Sullivans finally settled down for a much-needed sleep, and Barney dimmed the lights and ascended the stairs for the night. Tomorrow was another day; a day full of promise, and, for each of them, a life that would be changed forever.

Chapter 2

The Row

✦

Moquette Row (The Row) in North Yonkers, NY, is a cluster of attached housing units constructed between 1886 and 1889 by The Alexander Smith & Sons Carpet Company. The Row (as it was more commonly referred to) was intended to provide affordable living quarters for employees of The Carpet Shop. The Row's original design called for the construction of two parallel dead-end roads (Moquette Row North and Moquette Row South) that perpendicularly connected Nepperhan Avenue at their east end with Orchard Street at the west end.

The Carpet Shop was located on Nepperhan Avenue in North Yonkers, and *The Row* homes were located directly across the street from its main building. Moquette Row S and Moquette Row N consisted of twenty-one family units on both sides of each street totaling forty-two units per Row. Once completed, eighty-four units were available for employee rental.

Units on Moquette Road South were accessed from the west at Orchard Street. The east end of this road was blocked by a stone wall that housed a pedestrian staircase that descended to Nepperhan Avenue. Units on Moquette Road North were accessed directly from Nepperhan Avenue. The far end of this road also ended in a pedestrian staircase that ascended to Orchard Street.

Each two-story row house was approximately one thousand square feet, had four bedrooms (top floor), parlor, and eat-in dining/kitchen (main floor at street level), and one bathroom (cellar). Also included with each unit was a small private backyard. All homes and roads were maintained by Alexander Smith & Sons. Tenants paid approximately fourteen dollars a month.

For the new tenants, living in Moquette Row brought them one step closer to fulfilling their American dream. To move into a new, soundly constructed home that was spacious enough to accommodate their entire family was unfathomable. Since there were thousands of applications for this prime rental space, it was clear to them that they were selected and rewarded for their dedication and service to The Shop.

In addition to working at The Shop, Moquette Row tenants had much in common. Many were immigrants who migrated from Ireland and Scotland to work specifically at The Carpet Shop. With few exceptions, they were Roman Catholics who attended St. Joseph's Church and whose children attended St. Joseph's Grammar School. They were solid family members with accommodating personalities. Everyone in Moquette Row seemed to get along. The men would walk together to work, and the children would walk together to school.

Large families were not uncommon in the Row. There were always plenty of children at play, and they enjoyed sleighing in the winter, burning leaves in the fall, and swimming in the summer. On the warmer summer evenings, the woman would sit on front stoops and talk into the late evening hours. On the weekend men would gather to play cards, throw horse-shoes in the backyard and other seasonal recreational sports. The men were satisfied with their work environment; the women were satisfied with their living environment; the children were satisfied with their variety of friends. In The Row, they were all part of one large family, and residents looked out for each other. It was a wonderful place to live.

.   .   .   .   .   .

Number six's first tenant was John Carroll, who was born in Beacon, NY, on May 10, 1866. John was an employee of The Carpet Shop. When he moved into The Row on July 4, 1886, he brought his entire family, consisting of his brother (Barney), his mother Mary (Nana), and six siblings (Mary (Mom) being one of them). His father, Bernard Sr. died in 1884. When Mary (Mom) and her five children returned to The Row on November 13, 1911, only John, Barney, and Nana Carroll were still living there. Pop had died in 1894.

Bernard, Sr., (Pop) and Mary Carroll (Nana) were both born in Ireland, Pop in Cavan (County Roscommon) on January 12, 1839, and Nana in Elfin (County Roscommon) on August 6, 1836. As often was the case, they met in America in 1863 and married at St Joachim's R.C, Church, in Mattawan, NY, in August 1864. Pop immigrated to America in 1859 and joined the Union Army in 1861. He was granted a medical discharge in 1863. Nana immigrated in the 1850's. By trade, Pop was a painter. Nana worked as a domestic, cleaning the houses of the wealthier Yonkersonians.

After their marriage, the Carrolls settled in Beacon, NY. Shortly thereafter, they moved to Walnut Street in Yonkers. By the time they relocated to Moquette Row in 1886, the Carroll family had grown by seven children, the oldest being John. When they took residence, no one ever suspected that Six Moquette Row would remain as the Carroll family home for the next sixty-five years, and it remained so until June, 1952.

The Row was where Bernard Jr. (Uncle Barney), and Mary (Mom Carroll Sullivan) spent their teenage years together. Bernard Jr. (Barney) was born in Fishkill Landing, Beacon, NY, on August 10, 1875. Mary (Mom) was born in Beacon, on June 26, 1877. Her brother, John, was already twelve years old, and her brother, Barney, was three.

When Mary (Mom) and her five children returned to Six Moquette Row on November 13, 1911, she was returning to the home and the happy memories of her youth. She knew that the four bedrooms (two large, two small) on the second floor would provide sufficient sleeping accommodations for the expanded Carroll/Sullivan family. She also knew that the first-floor parlor and eat-in kitchen would be a family living areas. The one full bathroom located in the basement was inadequate but would just have to do.

To Mary (Mom), it was just like old times under some very difficult and stressful circumstances. She had shared many happy times in this house, and it always gave her great comfort when she returned for visits over the past ten years. The opportunity to raise her fatherless children in a loving family environment with her two older brothers as *surrogate fathers* was truly fortunate. She felt safe for the first time in a very long time. That night's sleep was the longest, deepest, and most restful she had had in years.

For the children, this was a wonderful adventure; for the adults it was a night of labor. Nana Carroll had already worked out the new-sleeping arrangements and had a list of furniture for her sons John and Barney to move. Nana would move into the smallest bedroom in the front of the house, and John and Barney would share the largest room on the front east side. For the time being Joseph, Vincent, little John, and their little sister, Mary would share the larger bedroom on the back east side. Mom and Arthur would be in a small room in the back of the house at the top of the stairs. When Arthur was older, he would join his brothers in the larger room, and little Mary would move in with Mom. Until the day Mom died (April 25, 1952), this would remain her bedroom.

While the boys helped their uncles carry furniture, little Mary clung tightly to Nana Carroll while Mom attended to Arthur. At 11 p.m., Barney insisted that the children go to bed. But sternness was not needed since all of the children had collapsed on one bed in the larger room as soon as they had finished moving furniture. Excitement or not, they were exhausted. The image of her four older children, still dressed in their winter coats, boots and hats, huddled together, and all sleeping on top of the covers was forever embedded in Mom's mind. That vivid memory gave her great comfort in her later years.

.   .   .   .   .   .

At 4 a.m. the next morning the Carrolls/Sullivans were awake again. It was Tuesday, November 14, 1911, the start of another workday. Nana was already in the kitchen preparing breakfast and lunch for her sons. Their shift at The Carpet Shop began at 5 A.M. and would last ten hours. However, of late, they were both working overtime, and she did not expect them home much before 7 p.m.

The cold outside had not subsided, but the heat that came from the coal-fired cooking stove in the kitchen warmed the entire house where openings (registers) in the ceiling in the first floor allowed the rising heat to warm the second floor. For Mom Sullivan and her children, who had grown accustomed to the cold, this was heaven. It had stopped snowing, but the ice-covered roads and sidewalks made traveling treacherous. With Nana Carroll's words of caution, John and Barney went off to work.

Nana had prepared a large pot of oatmeal that was simmering on the kitchen stove. The aroma of cinnamon permeated every room in the house. She did not expect to see anyone other than John and Barney this early in the morning, but she was pleasantly surprised to receive morning hugs from her grandsons, Joseph and Vincent, who were now washed and fully dressed.

"And where do you think you're off to at this time in the morning?" asked Nana with an elevated tone to her voice. "It's 4:30 a.m.!"

"Paper routes," replied Vincent. His face was just as serious as Nana's and his voice just as stern. "We each have our route, but we do them together and we get done faster."

"Yeah," added Joseph, "then we go to school. Let's eat."

Like their parents, the twins attended St. Joseph's Grammar School on St. Joseph's Avenue, about a half-mile from Nana's kitchen. Both were in the sixth grade, and they were excellent students. But it was clear to Nana that the twins had distinctly different personalities. Vincent was very serious about his responsibilities. Joseph, although just as responsible, was more laid back and let Vincent speak for him. Whereas Vincent would make things happen, Joseph would just let them evolve.

The twins continued that as soon as their brother John started school, he would also be able to help deliver the papers with them. They had it all figured out. Although unspoken, it was obvious that the sparse wages the twins earned were used to supplement the family's meager income. Knowing this saddened Nana but also warmed her heart. They were as giving and generous as their mother. There wasn't an ounce of selfishness in either of them.

"I hope it snows some more before school is out," added Vincent, "we will be able to shovel snow on the way home."

"Not me," said Joseph, "I need a break. We can shovel tomorrow."

"But it might melt by then," replied Vincent.

"Oh, OK," said Joseph, "If you shovel, I'll shovel."

And in that little exchange, Nana clearly understood the relationship between her twin grandsons.

As she easily identified the similarities between her sons, Barney and John, so she did her grandsons, Vincent and Joseph. Vincent was reserved and pensive like Barney, and Joseph was carefree and laissez-faire like John. She hoped that the grandchildren would enjoy the closeness that John and Barney shared. They were brothers and best friends. As it turned out, so were the twins.

"Well, don't do too much on your first day; your uncles may need your help carrying belongings from your mom's flat," chirped in Nana.

"I already spoke to Uncle John," said Vincent. "He said that if he needs our help, he will send a message to school for us. Joseph has a lot of junk, but I only have some clothes; Uncle Barney said we were going to get new stuff this weekend, anyway. So, I guess I don't have much to carry."

"Yup," said Joseph, "Uncle Barney said that we were going downtown to Sears & Roebuck. He said we might go on Saturday."

By 4:45 a.m. the twins had finished their breakfast and were bundling up to begin their work/school day. Little John and little Mary were still sleeping, and Mom Sullivan was just waking up. Arthur had just started fussing, and he was uncomfortable and hungry. The excitement of the prior evening had clearly disrupted his feeding schedule. Neither little Mary nor little John was old enough to attend school. John would begin next year, but Mary had a few years to go. They too would attend St. Joseph's.

At 5:45 a.m. there was a loud knock on the front door. The rapping at first startled Mom. But soon she realized that this was business as usual on

Moquette Row. Mrs. Glenn, Nana's next door neighbor, was at the front door. Both she and Nana attended 6:30 Mass at St. Joseph's Church every morning. Like the mailman, weather was neither an excuse nor a deterrent. By the time Mom answered the door Nana had put on her winter coat, winter boots, and was prepared for the half-mile uphill walk to St. Joseph's Church. Without another word, they were on their way. This routine would continue for the next ten years until failing health would greatly curtail Nana's activities.

As Mom and her brothers had agreed, she would spend her day attending to details. At 8:00 a.m., after Nana had returned from church, Mom placed her in charge of the little ones and began her walk to her first destination, the firehouse on Vineyard Avenue. This site was Patrick's last posting, and this is where many of his friends worked and congregated.

Captain Dorney was the first to greet her. He had been one of Patrick's pallbearers, along with Peter Conklin, who also greeted her with cheer and affection. Assistant Chiefs, Baker and Farrington, soon made their appearance and, before she knew it, Mom was surrounded by a mini legion of well-wishers. They all had questions about her and her children. Many had sent her food and clothing over the past few months. When Mary told them that she was moving to Moquette Row, they were relieved. Her short visit lasted an hour. When she left, she felt happy and refreshed.

Mom's next stop was the Lake Avenue Post Office. Having spent so much time at the firehouse, she knew she had to move a little faster. Arthur could be very demanding around feeding time. She hoped that she could complete change- of-address forms without further delay. Fortunately, the lines were short, and she finished in fifteen minutes. Soon she was on her way to the abandoned flat at 74 St. Joseph's Avenue.

Barney had asked her to return to her flat to pack up those belonging that she wanted transported to Moquette Row. She should put them in the front room, and he and John would retrieve them that evening. Since her flat was furnished as part of her rental agreement, she didn't own any furniture. Mom welcomed the opportunity to return to her apartment alone, not only to collect mementos of a former life but to spend a few moments of solitude in a place where she had been her happiest just a few years ago. It was there that she and Patrick had shared their special moments and future dreams. But destiny had other plans for her, and death had propelled her into a downward spiral that she was desperately struggling to reverse. She must be strong she reminded herself. That was a promise she made to Patrick when he first became ill, and that was a promise she was determined to keep.

Mom put documents, pictures, and clothing into a milk carton that she placed near the front door. There wasn't much, but its contents meant a great deal to her family. She gathered up whatever she could comfortably carry and bade farewell to the rooms she had once called home. Her brothers would retrieve the rest.

Mom then told her landlords, Margaret and Fred Wilson, that she would not need the flat any longer. The Wilsons lived in a first-floor apartment and were aware of the brothers' "rescue." The eight dollar rent was paid for the month of November, but Mom wanted Mrs. Wilson to feel free to rent it as soon as possible. The Wilsons were wonderful landlords, and she would miss them. They had both been so helpful and supportive in her time of need. Many times Margaret would babysit the children when Mom had to rush out to attend to other matters. She invited them to visit her at Moquette Row, and they encouraged her to return for a visit whenever she could. After a weepy, cordial farewell, Mom told them that her brothers would be back to collect her belongings. She was off again to her next stop.

A visit with Sister Mary Cecelia, the principal of St. Joseph's Grammar School, was her next order of business. The Sisters of Charity at St. Joseph's had been incredibly helpful, and Mom considered them family. In particular, Sr. Cecelia, who was less than five feet tall and almost as wide, was the consummate disciplinarian. Children feared her, and parents loved her... because their children feared her. She knew the entire Carroll family and had already spoken with Nana Carroll after Mass that morning.

Nana spoke to her with pride when she dramatized her sons' "rescue" of their little sister. Sr. Cecelia confided that she had spent many hours with Nana after Patrick's death and how greatly relieved Nana was to have her family back home with her. She believed that John and Barney would make excellent surrogate fathers. However, she did add, in a singsong voice, that Barney was a handful when he attended St. Joe's. Again Sr. Cecelia assured Mom that she would keep a close eye on her children and, as always, she would remember the entire family in her prayers. Mom was soon walking the short distance south on St. Joseph's Avenue to Ashburton Avenue.

Ashburton Avenue was the main east/west artery connecting Nepperhan Avenue to the east with North Broadway to the west. At its western end was the Hudson River. Although only a two lane road, Ashburton was the busiest street in Yonkers.

Lining both sides of Ashburton Avenue were three-story wood-structured buildings, the first floor being store fronts, and the second and third being apartments, often referred to as "cold water flats." These storefront structures extended from Nepperhan Avenue west to North Broadway. Beyond that point were the mansions of the Yonkers' wealthiest, which had a commanding view of the Hudson River.

Most of the flat tenants worked either on or near The Avenue (as Ashburton Avenue was traditionally called). Although it was primarily a retail shopping area, it was also a residential neighborhood unto itself. All of the merchants and tenants knew each other. They also knew their regular customers. Specifically, they knew Mary and Patrick Sullivan. In fact, many remember both when they were children growing up, some even attended their wedding, most attended Patrick's funeral. They all followed Patrick's baseball career and were affected in a very personal way when he died. In fact, Rusty's baseball picture still hung on the wall in Phillip's Barber Shop at the corner of Ashburton and Nepperhan. Mary felt at home on her frequent shopping trips to The Avenue.

For North Yonkers residents, The Avenue was a cornucopia for retail shopping needs. Whether it is for furniture, medical attention, shoe repair, laundry or yarn, The Avenue had it all. Fresh fruit and vegetables from the neighborhood farms were delivered every morning; fresh seafood, poultry, and various meats were delivered three times a week. Meat markets, vegetable stands, pharmacies, stationery stores, and numerous other businesses could be found on this half mile strip between Nepperhan Avenue and Broadway.

Credit was easily extended to regular customers, and merchants kept track of debts in a notebook that was normally kept in a drawer under the cash register. Like clockwork, stores opened at 7 a.m. and closed promptly at 7 p.m., six days a week. Sunday was a day of rest and worship. Nothing opened in Yonkers on the Sabbath other than houses of worship and the bakery.

At the center of Ashburton Avenue was St. Joseph's Church; to its east was Public Elementary School Number 12; to its west was Yonkers Homeopathic Hospital (more commonly called General Hospital). Further to the west was St. John's Convalescence Home. Vaccinations of all kinds were administered in the basement of St. Joseph's Grammar School. Regardless of what was going on in the world, everybody on The Avenue just seemed to get along. It was a true community. The cooperative spirit was infectious.

Above all, everybody treated the Sullivan children as their own. Rarely did the boys travel The Avenue without receiving a little candy or a very large ice-cream cone. Each merchant always told the children they were "putting it in the book," but, somehow, it never made it. When Mom tried to put a stop to these indulgences, her wishes were universally ignored. Ashburton Avenue was a very special place, and the Sullivan children were family.

One item on Mom's list was to settle her accounts with Norman, the Butcher, and Goodfriend's Grocery Story. On this matter, Mom stood firm. She knew to the penny how much she owed and would not accept a cent in charity. Once Frank Goodfriend tried to drop 75 cents from Mom's bill, and she could be heard chastising him all over The Avenue. Everyone knew that Mom Sullivan would pay her way; today wasn't any different. When Mom tried to tell the merchants that she had changed her mailing address, they already knew. Thanks to Nana Carroll, news traveled quickly on The Avenue. Nana loved to talk.

Finally, after what seemed like hundreds of conversations, Mom weaved her way home with a bag of freshly baked bread and stew meat for dinner. Nothing, yet everything, had changed for Mom. Instead of walking up St. Joseph's Avenue to her flat, she now walked down Ashburton Avenue and over Orchard Street to The Row. Whereas the former walk was one of loneliness, and despair; today's walk was one of optimism and elation. At 7 p.m., an exhausted family sat down for dinner.

By the time the meal ended, it was too late for John and Barney to return to Mom's apartment, so they postponed the trip to the next day. This was a reasonable decision and, besides, the evening was not a total loss. John once again assumed a leadership role and assigned responsibilities. Everyone would contribute something to help maintain the household. Joseph and Vincent would tend to the wood/coal box near the pot-bellied stove in the kitchen. Although Nana would keep the stove stoked, the older boys would eventually assume that responsibility.

Little John would care for Rex, the family dog. He would feed him in the morning and evening and put him in the backyard whenever necessary. John enjoyed the feeding but did not necessarily enjoy cleaning up after Rex. As little Mary grew older she would help him. If Rex needed to be walked on the street, either Uncle John or Barney would take him out.

The women would prepare the meals, clean house, and do the laundry. This was *the Irish way,* and the women welcomed the task. Nana, and, as it turned out, Mom, were excellent cooks, and they would share the meal preparation responsibilities. Little Mary would help with the kitchen chores and take on greater responsibilities as she grew older.

The men would be the bread winners with the bulk of the responsibility falling on Uncles John and Barney. The Sullivan boys would continue their paper routes, and they would shovel snow in the winter, and mow lawns when the summer months provided the opportunity to do so. The men would also do the heavy work around the house such as moving furniture, carrying groceries, carrying coal and wood. Only if there were a financial crisis would the women work.

The latter became a bone of contention for Mom Sullivan. She had always been fiercely independent and willingly accepted the financial responsibility of providing for her children. It was true that when she and Patrick married in 1899, she stayed home to raise the children. But when Patrick became ill with tuberculosis in 1908, financial necessity required that she work part-time at The Carpet Shop. When Patrick died, she became the sole provider for her five children, and she worked as often as circumstances enabled her to do so.

However, her brothers were also fiercely traditional and held strong to old school values. And those values dictated "a woman's place was in the home." They felt that they could earn enough to provide for her and her children without her contributing her meager earnings. They believed that in the long run, her continual presence at home was better for her children. They insisted, and rightfully so, that had Patrick lived, she would not be working.

The arguing had gone on for more than an hour before Nana Carroll settled it. She did not say much about family-management decisions. She usually left those matters to her very capable sons. But when she spoke, everyone listened. She was the ultimate traditionalist, so the brothers assumed that she would side with them and were anxious to hear what she had to say. But Mom was her pride and joy, and she admired her strength and independent streak. She also knew that no one was going to force Mom to do anything she chose not to do. She had a fiery temper and was just as likely to pack up her family and move back to St. Joseph's Avenue if her brothers' chauvinistic behavior continued. Nana felt that the conversation was heading dangerously in that direction. It was time for her sons to back off, and for her to intervene.

"Now children," Nana said calmly, "we do have a bit of a problem, do we not?" Everyone nodded in agreement.

"First, we all must realize that Mary is no longer the baby sister of the house. She is a mother and has handled a series of problems better than any man I know. She is a capable woman who does things on her own and in her way. Isn't this true John? You haven't been able to tell her what to do for twenty years now. And Barney, she has never listened to you at all. What makes you two think you can boss her around now?" The brothers began to fear that they were about to lose the argument.

Barney sat quietly in his chair at the far end of the kitchen table. He knew that Nana had made a decision that she was about to share. In the Irish way, the true leader of the household had emerged.

"Mary, while you are still nursing, wouldn't it be better for Arthur that you be rested and available to him?" She paused for a moment and continued, "and certainly little John has had enough disruption in his young life. At least for the time being he could use a little bit more attention." Again, Mom nodded in agreement. "Little Mary could also benefit from some private time from her mother. You've all been through a great deal, and it's time to take a deep breath before considering the next move."

"But Nana," she protested, "it is not right that my brothers should have to support my family."

"It's not right that they don't," retorted Nana, "it is our family too, and we are in this together. Your brothers just want to help, and their hearts are as big as they are. I am proud of them for stepping up. Their decision is based on love, Mary, not strength. No one intends to take away your independence, but the children need a mother and right now that is your role. Do you want them to be motherless and fatherless, too? Think child, put aside your stubbornness and tell me, what is the best for them?"

As tears began to form in Mom's hazel eyes, and gently roll down her cherubic cheeks, she lowered her head in acquiescence.

Nana continued, "Mary, will you agree that until Arthur stops nursing, and little Mary starts school, you will stay home to attend to the children? Mary nodded. "And boys, can we agree to discuss it again when Arthur reaches first grade?" John and Barney both nodded like little boys who had just received their first reprimand. Nana continued, "Now, I want you to promise that at that time if Mary decides to go to work, there will be no argument from you."

As the Carroll brothers nodded in the affirmative, Nana left the table. "Then it's done and I'll hear no more of it." The decision had been made. With that, she took her arthritic body to her stuffed chair by the front window. Although Nana's body was failing, her mind was not.

The Carroll children, having been sufficiently admonished, cleared the table and settled in for the night. However, Joseph and Vincent, who had silently witnessed the entire conversation, received their first lesson in diplomacy, *when the need for leadership is critical, the true leader will surface.* In this case, Nana's gentleness should never be confused for compliance. Leaders do not need to control everything, just the important things. This was a lesson that neither one would ever forget. Above all, their mother would be home with them, and that was all that mattered. By 10 p.m., the lights were out, and the family slept.

By Thursday, the weather had improved and was comfortably warmer. The icy streets were replaced by puddles of water and mud. Traffic, both automotive and pedestrian, had returned to normal, and Joseph and Vincent had a plan. As soon as school was out, they returned to the St. Joseph Avenue flat to collect their treasure box.

At 4 p.m., they entered the flat for the last time. Although it had been a place of happiness for their mother, it was a place of loneliness and fear for them. In their immediate memory, it was a place where their Dad had suffered and where he was eventually "waked." They could not rid their minds of the image of his lifeless body, dressed in his fireman's uniform and placed in a coffin that sat on a block of ice in their parlor. When they went to bed at night, they prayed that when they woke, their dad would be there. But deep down they knew those days were gone forever. When the mourners were gone, and his body was removed for the funeral and interment, it was as if life had ended for them. They were happy to leave the flat and return to the comfort of Moquette Row.

Among the items, their mother placed in the parlor was the box of family treasures. The box itself was actually an enclosed milk carton that their dad had put a lid on several years ago. In addition to containing many of the family legal documents (marriage and death certificates, baptism and communion certificates, etc.,), there were items that were very personal to them. A few pictures of their Mom and Dad were in a small manila envelope that had not been sealed. They looked at a baseball picture of Patrick, and they began to cry. And cry they did, long, hard, and together. It was the first tears they shared since the funeral, and it was a long overdue release that gave them strength to continue.

Among the treasures were their father's baseball glove, fireman's uniform, cap, helmet, and his treasured fireman's badge. His pocket watch was there along with his wedding ring. Vincent's taped covered baseball was there, and so was little Mary's tattered Raggedy Anne doll. At the bottom of the box was an iron statue of a chestnut stallion. The statue outweighed all of the other items in the treasure chest combined. Their dad called this horse "Dobbin." It was a souvenir that Pop Carroll brought home from the Civil

War. Dobbin was one foot high, one foot long and weighed more than 11 lbs. It was substantial. Although Pop Carroll seldom spoke of the war, he did say that Dobbin was the name of the stallion that his unit commander rode during the Battle of Fredericksburg. He said that this statue of that very brave warrior horse was a good reproduction.

For Joseph and Vincent, Dobbin was the physical manifestation of an imaginary friend. They each slept, played, spoke and dreamt with him at one time, or another. When Patrick and Mom married in 1899, Nana Carroll could not afford much, but she gave Dobbin to them as a wedding gift. For that reason alone, it held a very special place in their hearts. Although Dobbin was everyone's *special friend,* little John at age four was assigned by his dad to look after Dobbin while he was away from home recovering at a tuberculosis clinic in Raybrook, NY. Until little John died on September 8, 1985 (at age 80), he remained faithful to his pledge to take care of Dobbin. When he died, the caretaker responsibility was passed on to his son John Jr., who continued to care for Dobbin.

As darkness approached, the twins gathered up the *treasure chest,* bid farewell to the Wilsons, and headed to The Row. The box was heavy and even with both of them carrying it; it was a struggle, but they carried it together, a few steps at a time. They did not plan to leave any treasure behind. It was their legacy.

When they walked through the front door, Mom immediately noticed the box and knew exactly where her sons had been. She did not mention the treasure chest as she warmly greeted the twins and asked about their day. With little to say, they took Dobbin and placed him at the base of the artificial fireplace that sat on the east side of the kitchen wall (eventually he was moved to the living room). That was its original location prior to Mom and Patrick's wedding. When the family convened for dinner that evening, Uncle John was the first to notice Dobbin. "I see our old friend has come home to us," he said. "Welcome home, Dobbin!" In unison, Barney and Mom greeted their old friend in the same acknowledgment, "Welcome home, Dobbin!"

Unlike the night before, there was an air of frivolity in this evening's dinner conversation. John and Barney joked about an irrelevant work situation; Joseph and Vincent talked about school; little John asked questions about anything that popped into his head, and little Mary spoke to the Raggedy Anne doll that was in the treasure chest. Baby Arthur slept. Little Mary's reunion with her doll was very dramatic and heart-warming. As she told Raggedy Anne of her adventures during the past three nights, she also scolded her for not coming with her when they left the flat. As she chided Raggedy the family listened and laughed.

Towards the end of the meal, Nana noticed a distant look in Uncle John's eyes. She aptly identified his pensive mood (obviously triggered by Dobbin's return) as "John's mind being with the Leprechauns in Kilarney." John recalled the many conversations he had had with his father (Pop Carroll). With very little prodding, he began to speak about them.

He said that when Pop emigrated from Ireland to America at age twenty, he felt a great deal of anguish about leaving his family behind. And when he spoke of Ireland there was always a lilt to his voice and tears in his eyes. The only reason that Pop left Ireland was because he would have starved to death during the potato famine. When he had problems finding work in New York in the 1850's, he decided to seek his fortune in California; he changed his mind and enlisted in the Union Army when he reached Indiana. He enlisted on March 20, 1861. At that time, he was twenty years old; he was 5'7" tall, and had blue eyes and brown hair.

As an immigrant, Pop expected to face adversity and was prepared for it. But he was not prepared for the intensity of anti-Irish sentiment that he encountered, nor the difficulties of finding meaningful employment, not in the country that promised equality and opportunity for all. As he traveled west, he witnessed the frustrations of a country divided, and he felt compelled to get involved in the struggle. He decided that he would either leave America or take a stand against the secession movement. He chose the latter and joined the infantry as a member the Union's 14th Indiana Volunteer Regiment.

John continued, "As a soldier, he found friendship and acceptance. He acquired skills that he had never had before, and, above all, he felt that he was doing something productive to contribute to the betterment of his adopted country. He fought alongside his comrades at Winchester, Antietam, and Fredericksburg. When a debilitating condition known as "swamp fever" made it impossible for him to continue, he received a medical discharge on February 16, 1863. It pained him to leave his friends and the Union army. Dobbin was a reminder to him of all that he believed in."

The return of Dobbin to the Carroll kitchen triggered John's memories of his father. He continued, "Abraham Lincoln was Pop's hero and one time he actually got close enough to shake his hand. Another time *Old Abe* even waved to him. Pop was saddened by Lincoln's assassination and talked of the despondency in the land after Lincoln's death, and the resurgence of hatred for the south."

As John shared his memories, the entire family sat mesmerized by the family history lesson they were receiving. Pop Carroll was a very private man, and in many ways he was an enigma to his family. Through John's sharing his memories, they acquired a better understanding of the man who was becoming less of a mystery. At 10 p.m., everyone retired to bed. He had given them plenty to think about.

It wasn't until bedtime that Mom realized that John and Barney had not retrieved the remaining belongings in the St. Joseph's flat. She decided that if her brothers couldn't do it, she would. Apparently John was thinking the same thing because he visited her just before she fell asleep to tell her that he and Barney would collect them the next evening. Mom was running out of school clothing for the children, and the situation was getting critical.

Dinner was early on Friday and by 6 p.m., John and Barney set out for St. Joseph's Avenue. Much to Mom's chagrin, they returned empty-handed three hours later. When Mom asked them if they went to the apartment, they sheepishly said that they had. She asked them if they had any difficulties; they said that they had not. When she asked what happened to her belongings, they were both mute. When she asked again, Barney began to waffle. This hesitation was a signal for Mom to go into the attack mode because she knew something had happened that she would not be happy about. However, before she could strike, John again stepped up.

"Mary," he said, "We looked at the clothing and realized that they would not do for our nephews and niece; or, for that matter, our sister. Some we gave away to our new friend, Peter Finch, but the bulk we threw away; actually, we burned them. And you no longer have a winter coat, either. In fact, all your clothing is gone. Saturday we are all going shopping and our family will no longer look like a bunch of *rag pickers*. You and the children are getting new clothing for a new beginning."

A shocked Mom Sullivan sat down in the closest chair. In disbelief she said, "You did what? Have you two gone completely loony? We are out of clothes!"

"Don't worry about the cost, Mary," piped up Barney when he saw a look of terror on his sister's face, "We will keep track of the cost for new clothing, and you can pay us back when you go back to work after Arthur starts first grade." That being said, Barney starting laughing hysterically. As he laughed and as he talked, he confessed that his greatest thrill was burning Mary's clothes.

Next, John chimed in to calm down Barney, but he started laughing, too. Soon, the brothers were out of control. As Mom asked if they had a *wee bit of the spirit,* they confessed that they did stop at Bronkey's Tavern on their way to and from the flat. Bronkey's was a half-mile away, in the wrong direction. The more they tried to explain how they ended up there, the harder they laughed. Soon, although she didn't know exactly why, Mom also broke into uncontrollable laughter. It had been a decade since Nana Carroll had heard such goings on in her house, and it sounded good!

Mom Sullivan knew that her children needed new clothing and that her winter coat was not fit even for charity. She had long ceased to be embarrassed because there was nothing she could do about it. But she never suspected that even in their wildest moments her brothers would burn it. She had all she could do to survive. Anything other than someone's *hand-me-downs* was a luxury that she could not afford.

She also realized that her brothers had outsmarted her. She was the one who pushed for a work agreement, and they were pretending that it would happen. Her brothers were doing what Patrick would have done. The boys' poverty clothing was an embarrassment to all of them. Although they never complained, it was something that had to be corrected. Any further laundering would add to the erosion of the fabric. When it came to shoes, no longer would cardboard inserts cover up the holes in the soles. Her brothers' assessment was right on target, and she had no rejoinder. Besides, they had already disposed of the clothing. She didn't have a choice.

"Ok," she responded, "tomorrow we go shopping, but we will keep track of every cent, and we won't go overboard."

"Agreed," said Barney. "Tomorrow we are going shopping, and we'll let little Arthur keep track of the money." Again, John and Barney broke into uncontrollable laughter. Before Mom could object, the brothers were gone.

"I do have a question to ask both of you," Mom shouted to their backs. How is it that Joseph and Vincent knew that they were going shopping last night, and I'm just finding out about it today?"

In the amicable way a cat behaves after eating the canary, John replied, "Don't you know sister that I have very smart nephews?"

"Yes," interjected Mom, "and they have uncles who kissed the Blarney Stone."

To Mom, it was clear that her brothers had assumed a fatherhood role for her children, and this was something that they surely needed. She decided that at least for a time they could be spoiled. Certainly, they deserved something special in their lives. And she could do with a bit of pampering herself. At least for awhile she would just let things evolve in a normal way. The brothers needed children in their lives, and her children needed a father in theirs. And that is exactly how the relationships evolved. And besides, a little laughter never hurt anyone.

Early Saturday morning John, Barney, Joseph, Vincent, little John, little Mary and Mom boarded the Nepperhan Avenue Number 5 trolley for their trip to Getty Square. Excitement was in the air. Arthur would remain with Nana. On their way out the door, Mom saw Nana slip John an envelope that she knew contained some money. She accurately deduced that this was a secret contribution to the family shopping spree. She pretended not to see. Everyone was excited about this grand adventure, everyone except Arthur, who was sleeping soundly in his crib. Mom considered asking John, who was going to keep track of the money, but she decided to leave well enough alone. Obviously it couldn't be Arthur.

Nana, who had been in on the scheme all along, had also provided a shopping list of what was needed for the children. Mom was not included on this list, but it was assumed that she would also come home with a complete wardrobe since her brothers burnt all her clothing.

Beginning with undergarments, each would receive three sets. For shoes, each would receive two pairs, one for play and one for Sunday Mass. A dozen pairs of socks and stockings accompanied the shoes. Three pairs of play pants and shirts plus two sweaters for all were next on the list. In addition, each received one dress outfit to complement the dress shoes. Joseph and Vincent received three winter coats to share, little John and little Mary each received two. Two winter hats, one for play and one for dress, two scarves and three pairs of gloves each and six shirts for the boys made for a complete purchase of the essentials. A variety of belts, suspenders, knickers, clip ties, etc., added the final touches.

Little Mary received an equal complement of girl's clothing, and they all selected something for Arthur. Barney insisted that the children and Mom throw what they were wearing away before they left the store. The past was behind them, and they were dressing for the future; they were wearing new clothing home. Mom immediately complied because, as she later told Nana, "My brothers are so crazy these days, God only knows what they would have done if I refused." The children loved the idea and gladly shed what they had come to call their "rag picker clothes."

The uncles were giddier than Santa Claus on Christmas Eve. Frugal Mom tried to object from time to time, but her words were drowned out by the excitement of her children. The children and their uncles were having the time of their lives. When the uncles disagreed about a particular selection, one choosing one item over another, they bought both. When they left Genung's Department Store and Sears & Roebuck, they were so overloaded with packages that they couldn't possibly carry all of them home. They left whatever they couldn't carry with store security. They planned to return Monday to claim the remaining purchases. This time they would return. The Sullivan children and their mother would be the best-dressed *rag pickers* on The Row.

Just for good measure, when they left the shopping area, they purchased a new winter coat for Nana. Unknown to each, Barney bought a new winter hat for John, and John bought new winter gloves for Barney. That would be the biggest surprise for both when they all arrived home.

The happiness that night at Moquette Row was infectious. The children were going to look and dress like other children, and Mom was going to be warm and in style. She had insisted that her clothing be the color black that signaled a widow in mourning. For the remainder of her life, as fashions and styles changed, Mom continued to wear black. In the euphoria of the moment, they had almost forgotten about Patrick. The brothers respected her wishes, as long as her new outfits were fashionable, and they were. When the entire family attended 6:30 Mass on Sunday morning, they were a picture of fashion and design. And this is exactly the way Patrick would have wanted it to be.

Chapter 3

The Most Wonderful Time of the Year

✦

By mid-November 1911, the Carroll/Sullivan family had established a daily routine that worked for them. Nana Carroll would arise at 4 a.m. and prepare breakfast for the household and box lunches for her sons, John and Barney. In concert with the season, breakfast would vary from hot oatmeal, bread, juice milk or tea, and cinnamon buns during the colder months to fresh fruit, eggs, bacon, and warm bread during the warmer weather. The meals would vary, but the timeline did not. The family would always wake up to an enticing aroma signaling that Nana Carroll was in the kitchen.

By 5 a.m. Uncles John and Barney left for work. They were both on the morning shift at The Alexander Smith Carpet Company (The Shop). The twins, Joseph and Vincent, would soon join her for their breakfast. At 5:30 a.m. they would complete their household chores and leave to deliver newspapers on their way to school. At 6 a.m. Nana would begin her 30 minute walk to morning Mass at St. Joseph's R.C. Church on Ashburton Avenue (The Avenue). Rain or shine, warm or cold, the thought of Nana missing Mass was unacceptable. At the same time, Mom would be tending to Arthur. He, too, was an early riser. Little Mary and little John would sleep until 7 a.m., rising just in time to greet Nana as she returned from Mass. In later years, the family would look back on these mornings as the perfect way to start the day. By 7:30 a.m. they were all focused, fed and prepared to face any challenge that might present itself.

Little Mary was her mother's helper. She especially enjoyed fussing over her baby brother, Arthur, who was only a few months old and barely visible under the blue blanket that swaddled him. She would tickle him and make funny faces for him, bring her mother cotton balls, diapers, and any other item she needed. She even sang silly songs to keep Arthur entertained. She continually questioned her mother about Arthur, whom she treated as her very own living doll. Yes, except when Arthur cried, she preferred him over Raggedy Anne whom she had not yet forgiven for remaining in the St. Joseph flat when the rest of the family took *the rescue walk* to Six Moquette Row a week ago.

The adjustment for little John was not as seamless. In fact, he was a nudge who just seemed to be in the way all the time. For instance, he would feed and put Rex out in the gated backyard but forget to bring him back inside. Or, he would tie a string around Rex's tail with a bell attached to the other end. This prank caused a disruption wherever Rex went. It was particularly annoying when little John would have Rex run up and down the hallway stairs. Then there were his and Rex's adventures in the coal bin (which had become their personal fortress), inevitably requiring a bath for both and additional laundering of his clothing.

When little John wasn't causing mischief, he was constantly attaching himself to Nana Carroll, who would eventually lose patience with his antics. By the time Uncle John and Barney returned home from work, they were exhausted and wanted to eat and rest. But little John wanted to wrestle, play catch or any other game that would satisfy his need for their attention. Little John had boundless energy, and that was becoming a problem.

·   ·   ·   ·   ·   ·

While each member of the Moquette Row family was transitioning to a new lifestyle, the excitement of the forthcoming holiday season seemed to be everywhere. Tuesday, November 21, 1911, started out like every other morning. It was cold when the Sullivan twins left Moquette Row at 5:30 a.m. The recent snowfall had made walking perilous; the overhanging mist diminished visibility. But the brothers were wearing their new winter outfits, and they were impervious to the prevailing weather conditions. They collected their bundles of papers (The Yonkers Herald) at the intersection of Moquette Row and Orchard Street and divided them according to their designated responsibilities. Vincent delivered to Moquette Row North, and Joseph delivered to Moquette Row South. They both shared Orchard Street between Moquette Row and Ashburton Avenue. They met at the intersection of Orchard Street and Ashburton Avenue and walked west on Ashburton together to St. Joseph's Grammar School on St. Joseph's Avenue.

But when they reached The Avenue, they noticed significant changes to the landscape. For instance, cardboard figures of turkeys, pilgrims, and

Indians were looking out from every store window. They also noticed the unusually large number of fresh food delivery wagons that lined both sides of the overcrowded street. In particular, caged live turkeys and chickens were in abundance and very noisy. Hundreds of delivery men carried fresh meat and produce into the markets, and early morning shoppers were assembling in anticipation of the official store openings at 7 a.m. There was an excitement in the air as hundreds of adults rushed to and fro without any particular pattern or purpose. The Avenue was more congested and the people more animated than anyone had ever seen.

Joseph and Vincent immediately recognized another chance to contribute to their new household. The holidays meant new employment opportunities, and they meant to take advantage of that. They systematically canvassed merchants on both sides of The Avenue asking if they would be doing any additional hiring for the season. By the time they reached St. Joseph's Grammar School, they both had lined up after school and weekend jobs right up to Christmas Eve. The merchants realized that the twins would be reliable and put their extra earnings to good use.

When they arrived at school, they saw another change in routine. Sr. Loretta Vincent was directing all children to go to the school basement where they were to line up before reporting to assigned classrooms. Normally, the children would assemble in the school courtyard where they would be subdivided by grade, gender, and height (shortest in front). Once they were all accounted for (no talking please), they marched into the building and their respective classrooms. However, Sr. Cecilia felt that it was too cold for the children to remain outside; so they would report directly to the basement when they arrived at school until further notice.

.   .   .   .   .   .

At home, the falling snow turned *The Row* into a winter wonderland. Dozens of children of all ages took full advantage of this transient utopia. Children would rush home from school, take out their sled (The Flyer), and ride from the top of Moquette Row at Orchard Street, down to the staircase at the bottom. A decline of 33 % was very steep, making for a very exciting ride. The older children and parents would construct snow barriers at the bottom to prevent sleigh riders from flying over the pedestrian steps onto Nepperhan Avenue, a drop of about 15 feet.

The older children were more adventurous than, the younger ones. They would pull their sleds up the hills to Ridge Avenue (two blocks north-west of Orchard Street), and then sleigh ride down past Glenwood and Orchard Streets to Orchard Place, finishing their mile and a half jaunt at Nepperhan Avenue. Along the way they would dodge cars, horse drawn wagons, and, once they reached Nepperhan Avenue, trolley cars. From there, they would walk south to Moquette Row and begin the cycle again.

Efforts on the part of Yonkers Public Works Department to put sand on the hills with their horse-drawn sand-wagons were greatly impeded by an entire neighborhood of outraged children. More often than not, the employees' efforts were thwarted, and sanding activities were curtailed to the evening hours, when children were sleeping. Inclement weather was a parent's nightmare but a child's dream.

Big things were also happening within Six Moquette Row. When Joseph and Vincent arrived home from school on November 21, they were greeted with an aroma that meant that cookies were being baked in the kitchen. But what they discovered was much more. The sweet smell of sugar cookies joined with the aroma of baked wheat bread. The blend was magnificent. As Vincent entered the kitchen, he noticed that Nana was just removing a pumpkin pie from the oven and placing it on the table to cool. Simultaneously, Mom was placing an apple pie into the same oven. Nana announced that a mince pie would be next. Their little kitchen smelled like Miller's Bakery.

The small kitchen floor was covered with groceries-celery, carrots, potato sacks, turnips, tomatoes, lettuce, and so many other items that neither twin even knew the name. There wasn't a safe place to walk without stepping on something.

"What's going on?" inquired a very surprised Joseph. He had never seen so much food in one place in his entire life.

"Thanksgiving," said Nana, "We are having Thanksgiving dinner here for our family and some friends. Have you forgotten that it's just two days away? Didn't little John tell you that this was a day of celebration?"

"Yes," said Joseph, "but he didn't say we were feeding all of Moquette Row."

"Well, not everyone," replied Nana, "but this year we have a lot to be thankful for, and it's time for some good cheer. We are healthy and together, the worst is over for our family, and life will just keep on getting better. On Thanksgiving morning, we are all going to 6:30 Mass, including little Mary, little Arthur, and even Uncles John and Barney. It's high time we give thanks for what we have and stop regretting the things we don't."

The thought of Uncles Barney and John going to church was a frightening one for the Sullivan children. They recalled a dinner conversation not so long ago when Nana attempted to get her recalcitrant sons to attend Sunday Mass. They proclaimed that if they were to enter St. Joseph's Church together, the entire building would collapse around them. Apparently, Nana was convinced that this would happen because she immediately stopped her assault. But their uncles' comments did make a lasting impression on them.

However, this time Nana was determined. Her plan for a family outing to church was more of a "command performance" than a request. When the uncles alluded to the collapsing church scenario, Mom replied that the uncles would enter first and, if the church remained stable, then the rest of the family would follow.

Nana noticed a puzzled expression on Joseph's face. "I know what you are thinking Joseph," continued Nana, "We all miss him. But your dad would have been the first one out the door and up to the altar. We mean no disrespect; we are celebrating the lives and joy he gave us while he was here. We are thankful to him, and to the Lord. Plus, he always loved the holidays."

At 4 o'clock Thanksgiving morning, the entire household was up and preparing to leave. Nana Carroll insisted on a 6 a.m. departure and at 6 a.m. they all walked out the door, and, as Mom later recalled, they were "dressed to the nine." By 6:20 the Carroll/Sullivan family was seated in the front pew of St. Joseph's Church. Much too little John's dismay, sitting behind them was Sr. Cecelia and a dozen Sisters of Charity. Little John, who is normally fidgety in church, never even moved a muscle. Baby Arthur slept soundly while little Mary snuggled in between Nana and Mom.

Clearly, Uncles John and Barney were not the model parishioners. But they were embarrassed when Fr. Reed while giving his homily paid particular attention to the Carroll/Sullivan family with a special blessing. He then mentioned that it had been a long time since he had seen Uncles John and Barney at Mass. Vincent and Joseph knew precisely what Fr. Reed meant and started laughing. Little john was too frightened to move. Nana gave her sons an "evil eye" and Mom gave a broad smile. But nothing matched the bright red complexion of Uncles John and Barney. They looked like they were about to explode and were the first out the door when the Mass ended. Nothing was said about the homily when they returned to Moquette Row, but everyone knew what Fr. Reed meant.

Once home, the boys delivered papers, and John and Barney went to the basement to retrieve the two 22 lb. turkeys given to them by The Carpet

Shop. The ladies of the house began preparations for the 3 p.m. family feast. Whenever anyone attempted to sample a cookie or piece of the pie, Nana Carroll went on the attack. Yes, there was probably enough to, as Barney complained, "feed an army," but Nana was emphatic that no one was going to touch the food until the company arrived. The excitement in the air was infectious and, as the noon hour came and went, it began to build.

By connecting odd tables and chairs from around the house, and borrowing tables from the neighbors, the dinner table extended from the front parlor wall to the far end of the kitchen, a distance of about 20 feet. It was set to accommodate 24 people. The smells from the kitchen were driving Uncle Barney to distraction, and he decided he was going out for a walk.

"If you be going to Bronkey's for a bit of the spirit, don't come back. I'll have none of that today," shouted Nana.

"Now, don't you be worrying about Barney," said Uncle John, "I'll go with him to make sure he doesn't get into any trouble."

"You will not," said Mom, "You promised to take the boys sledding, and they are waiting outside for you."

With that, Uncle John and Barney headed for the back door. But it was blocked by Nana who already had Barney's gloves in her hand.

"Now, don't you be disappointing your nephews," shouted Nana, "bad enough what they heard in church today. Now be off with the both of you."

The contrite uncles joined their nephews on the sidewalk and headed for the top of The Row. Uncle John was overheard commenting to Barney that "they should have left two days before and just showed up for dinner." He didn't appreciate Fr. Reed's comments.

At 2 p.m., company began to arrive, just moments after the three brothers and their uncles returned to the house, covered with snow. Mom quickly whisked them to the basement where they could remove their wet coats and boots. The loud joking that could be heard even on the top floor was a clear indicator of the wonderful time they had.

Mom asked herself "How can I be angry at those two overgrown galoots? They are the best thing for the children right now. They make them laugh! They make all of us laugh." She vowed to be less critical of their antics.

As the company arrived, the Sullivan brothers (excluding Arthur) were there to greet them. They took wet clothing from the guests and brought them to the basement to dry. Dry clothing was placed on the beds on the second-floor. Wet boots and shoes remained in the first-floor hallway. Rex, the dog, did not take kindly to the company and hid under the bed in Nana Carroll's room for the entire day. The boys were perfect gentlemen, stayed in the thick of the day, and enjoyed every moment of it.

Although Mom knew all of the guests, her children did not. They were thrilled at the attention and pennies they received from their new-found relatives, Uncle Tommy, Aunts Sarah and Catherine. The Drexlers from next door came with their two children (Gus and Ellen), and the Maxwell's from the North Row joined them with their three children, Mary, Margaret, and John. Even though the Maxwell children were Protestants and attended Number 9 Public School, they played with the Sullivan boys all the time. Little John always denied having special feelings for little Mary (Mae) Maxwell because they were about the same age. But those suspicions were eventually confirmed seventeen years later when they married on June 26, 1928. They remained best friends and partners until John's death on September 8, 1985. They had been married for 57 years, and neither one had ever dated another person. Their love affair lasted 74 years, and, in all probability, resumed in paradise after Mary's (Mae's) death on December 29, 1991.

At 3 p.m., all guests were called to the table, grace was offered by little John and just before the meal began, Barney asked for a moment of silence in memory of Patrick Sullivan. Although unexpected, Mom appreciated her brother's intentions and offered a toast appropriate for the holidays; after which she directed the gathering to "dig in."

Few have ever seen a table as full and rich with the variety of food that this one had. It seemed like there was an unending supply of everything imaginable. There were sweet potatoes and potato balls, creamed turnips, cheese, celery, apple bread, cranberry jelly, figs, turkey with an abundance of both white and dark meat. John Maxwell, Sr., had been assigned to carve the turkeys. Since he also worked at The Carpet Shop, he, too, was given a turkey, which he brought to the Carrolls, making it a total of three turkeys or 66 lbs of turkey meat. There were three varieties of breads, some dumplings, and garden salads that Aunts Catherine and Sarah contributed. Gravy and butter plus other unnamed foods found their way to an already overcrowded table. There were cider, milk and soda water for the women and children and *special cider* just for the men.

After the main meal had been finished, desserts were served. Although most proclaimed that they "could not eat another thing," they changed their minds when they saw the apple, pumpkin and mince pies. For those who were not interested in pie, there was pudding and tutti frutti ice cream. An hour later, some went for a walk; the men smoked cigars, and the others just collapsed in their chairs from the weight of overeating.

Vincent found the meal to be confusing. Even at age 11 it was clear that he had a mathematical mind and that he also loved turkey legs. However, at the table at least ten guests proclaimed that they, too, wanted legs. With only three turkeys, Vincent calculated that there would only be six legs. But to his surprise, Mom produced a leg for anyone who wanted one. When Vincent asked her afterward how she did that she told him, it was a secret that she would tell him when he was older. When Mom passed in 1952, she took the secret of the multiplying turkey legs to the grave with her. All that was known was that year after year, whoever wanted a turkey leg at Thanksgiving or Christmas at Mom Sullivan's house could count on getting it.

It was after 8 p.m. when all the guests went home. After the meal, the children played games around the house, and the adults sat and talked. And while they talked, they cleaned up the mess that a large meal for twenty-four people had generated. The men folded the chairs and tables and returned them to their prior locations. The women tended to the kitchen, washing the floor, counters, dishes, pots, and pans. By 9 p.m., Six Moquette Row was back to normal. The Sullivan children could not remember ever having such a wonderful time. They would be certain to tell Rex about it as soon as he came out from under Nana's bed.

After the company had left, Nana and Mom realized that they had a storage problem with the extra food. Their little ice-box was filled to the brim, and the basement storage area was not cold enough to sustain the large quantity of cooked food for an extended period. Their dilemma was to decide what to do with the surplus food this late in the evening.

As Nana said, "It would be a sin to throw all this food away."

Mom agreed but believed it was too late to start distributing food to the neighbors, who probably had enough leftovers of their own.

John Carroll, who had overheard the conversation, told the ladies to "box the food," he had a solution.

Within minutes John, Barney and the twins appeared in the kitchen fully dressed in warm winter clothing. There were five boxes of food on the kitchen table. The twins each took the smaller ones; Barney carried two, and John took the heaviest.

As they walked out the front door, Uncle John announced that they would be back in a "little bit of time." They were gone before Nana could ask them where they were going but she assumed they were off to St. Joseph's Rectory for Fr. Reed to distribute the leftovers.

When they returned within the hour, Mom was about to ask where the food had disappeared to, but Joseph answered the question before it was asked.

"Peter Finch and his friends said to tell you Thank You and Happy Thanksgiving."

Nothing more needed to be said. This was the Sullivan way.

.   .   .   .   .   .

By the end of November, Nana spent more exhausting days with little John than she could tolerate and decided to speak with Mom about him.

"Mary," she said, "Did you notice that John can count to fifty, and he knows what those numbers mean?"

"Yes," replied Mary, "and he also knows the alphabet and can read small words. Joseph and Vincent play words games with him and tell him stories about school. I don't know how much he can read, but I do know he loves numbers. In fact, just yesterday he told me he wants one more sister, two more brothers, and another uncle just for himself. He said that this would make "four" more family members."

As Nana and Mom laughed, Nana said, "I believe the boy is bored and should be in school."

"I agree Nana, but he's too young and can't start until next year."

"Have you thought about speaking to Sister Cecelia about him," asked Nana.

"No, Nana, but I suspect that you have," replied Mom, "What did you, and she have to say about little John?"

"Not too much! But she speaks to me almost every day after Mass about the children, and I've been telling her that he is very bright and needs something to keep him busy. Just this morning she suggested that you bring him to school tomorrow, and she would talk with him."

The next day (Friday, December 1, 1911) Nana, Mom, Sr. Cecelia, and little John met. Sr. Cecelia spoke with John at length, questioning him about words, numbers, the importance of being good, and things that made him happy. He seemed happiest when he was with his two older brothers. His sad times were when everyone was too busy to play with him. But what impressed Sr. Cecilia the most was his clarity of thought, his vocabulary, and his ability to articulate his feelings. He seemed childish until he was forced to focus on a specific topic. Then, he seemed to be much older than his six years. On Monday, December 4, little John became a member of Miss Blue's first-grade class. John was the youngest of the forty-one students in the room.

Little John was petrified of Sr. Cecelia and much too frightened to become a discipline problem. So, from that day forward he went with Vincent and Joseph, helped deliver papers, and attended school. Above all, he avoided Sr. Cecilia at any cost. Almost eight years later, when he graduated from St. Joseph's Grammar School, he still hid whenever he saw her. Clearly her first impression was a lasting one.

John quickly adapted to first grade and loved to play act. His budding theatrical career was jump started by the fourth-grade teacher, Mrs. McQuade. She was in charge of student performances and cast him in the role of the *littlest pilgrim* in a post-Thanksgiving Day play that was attended by the entire school. John was thin as a rail, less than three feet tall, had freckles, a cherubic face, stick-out ears, intense hazel eyes, and red hair. He was "adorable", or so Mrs. McQuade thought. He was a hit in his first performance. Although his part was a non-speaking one, he seemed at ease on the stage, and it appeared that this was the beginning of a budding thespian future.

Joseph and Vincent were proud brothers when little John made his acting debut. However, his fame was short-lived. In his second role as Tiny Tim in the annual performance of <u>A Christmas Carol</u> a few weeks later, he not only forgot his lines, but he also made matters worse by jumping off the shoulders of Bob Cratchet because he had to go to the bathroom. When Mom Sullivan (who was backstage) saw John running to her holding his crotch with a pained expression on his face, she quickly whisked him off to the boys' bathroom. When John finished and while Mom was re-buttoning his pants, he ran out the door and back onto the stage, where he was warmly greeted with extended applause, hilarious laughter, and a standing ovation. This performance ended his acting career.

The incident was reported but not ever discussed again at the Moquette Row dinner table. But Vincent did tell little John that he could not participate in any more plays until he and Joseph graduated eighth grade.

From John's first day of school, he became a font of information at the family dinner table. He never stopped talking about all the new things he was learning. He even stunned Uncle Barney when he announced that Abraham Lincoln said he didn't have to go to school on Thanksgiving Day. Apparently, Miss Handrahan had given her class a brief history lesson and announced that Lincoln established Thanksgiving as a national holiday. After hearing this revelation, little John, spread the word. No one could convince John that Lincoln didn't say anything about school. As far as he was concerned, Abe was OK with him. Each evening he had a new story and a new area of excitement. Nana wondered what the family would do for dinner entertainment when summer vacation arrived, and her grandson was back to being a nudge.

During the first week in December, the landscape between Orchard Street and St. Joseph's Avenue began to change again. The cardboard turkeys that appeared in some merchant windows were replaced by thousands of paper representations of Santa Claus. Some were tall, and some were small, and some were heavy, and some were thin, but all had an elderly gentleman with a white beard, carrying an oversized bag that was stuffed with toys. Unlike Thanksgiving where only a smattering of stores displayed the turkey, Santa appeared in virtually every storefront. In most cases, banners wishing passers-by a Merry Christmas and a Happy New Year were also strung high and low.

Street lamps and doorways were draped with garlands, and paper Christmas trees; candy canes, reindeer, and snowflakes were hung in equal sections across Ashburton Avenue from its base at Nepperhan Avenue all the way west to North Broadway. Above the stores, many of the tenement windows displayed wreaths and candles. Store windows were painted with Christmas scenes, encouraged by the annual window-painting competition among school children. To the Sullivan brothers, The Avenue had been transformed into a Magical Kingdom.

The Nativity display that graced the small front lawn of St. Joseph's Rectory on Ashburton Avenue was one of majesty and splendor. The three foot statues of the Three Wise Men, along with camels, sheep, and mules, all circled those of Joseph and Mary, who were placed in a wooden manger to await the arrival of the Baby Jesus on Christmas Eve. The inside of St. Joseph's Church was equally grandiose, with a duplicate nativity scene and hundreds of wreaths, candles, poinsettias, and religious artifact.

On Christmas Eve, all statue figures were replaced with live elementary school children who played various roles in the Nativity pageant. Little John expressed an interest in being one of the wise men but lost it very quickly when he learned that Sr. Cecilia was interviewing students for the various roles. The mere mention of Sr. Cecilia was enough to discourage him from volunteering his services.

On Ashburton Avenue, horse-drawn wagons and carriages were adorned with sleigh bells and wreaths. Some even had stuffed figures that looked like real people, wearing red clothing and propped up in the wagon's passenger seat to look like Santa. The loud ringtones from the various sounding bells and chimes filled the avenue with a cacophony of beautiful sounds. It seemed that wherever one went, they were greeted with "well wishers" bidding a hearty Merry Christmas and Happy New Year to all. On the evening of December 22, Christmas Carols were scheduled to be sung around the big Christmas tree in Manor House Square in downtown Yonkers. The Carroll/Sullivans planned to attend.

Little Mary Sullivan was particularly fascinated by the spectacle of the holiday celebration. Since she did not attend school as of yet, she did not see the sights her brothers saw. So, when on Friday, December 22, the extended family made the two-mile trek from Moquette Row to Manor House Square, she was totally captivated by what she was seeing and hearing. The sights and sounds of the season were everywhere. Christmas music, Christmas bells, and seasonal greetings filled the air and this added to her excitement. The walk was much slower than usual because Nana Carroll insisted on joining the family on this adventure, and John and Barney insisted, "We're a family, and we will walk together." Little Mary and her brothers would anxiously run ahead and then walk back as her brothers pointed out to her the various sites along the way. The entire family was dressed in their finest new winter clothing.

The family stopped momentarily to join in with the carolers in front of St. Joseph's Church, but they saved most of their voices and enthusiasm for Manor House Square. They purchased hot chocolate and apple cider from a street vendor at the intersection of Ashburton and Palisade Avenue. By the time they resumed their excursion to Manor House Square, the streets had become very crowded with thousands of happy and good natured people who were all heading in the same direction.

They arrived at Manor House Square just as the ceremony began, and for two straight hours they sang and re-sang classical Christmas Songs, ending the evening with a very solemn rendition of *Silent Night*. Music books were distributed throughout the crowd, but it did not appear that anybody needed one. Just as *Silent Night* ended, Santa arrived in a two-horse-drawn carriage, led by the City of Yonkers' first gasoline-powered fire truck. With sirens sounding and horns honking and spectators cheering, Santa circled the crowd, eventually disappearing into the trolley garage on the corner of Buena Vista and Main Street, after which, the crowd dispersed.

In his travels, Santa threw candy to the crowd, and the Sullivan twins made sure they collected enough for the entire family. The twins fussed over Mary, and she was in her glory. Mom remained in the background. Patrick's memory was always with her, but she vowed to grieve in private and struggled to keep it so.

Little Mary was the first to tire and asked Uncle Barney to carry her. As he swooped her up in his massive arms, he was the picture of fatherly pride. She promptly snuggled close to his warm body and fell asleep. Shortly thereafter, little John began to show signs of fatigue. But before he asked (he was too proud to admit that he was tired to his brothers), Uncle John picked him up and placed him on his shoulders. This elevation gave the *wannabe thespian* another chance to perform as he shouted to anyone who would listen, "God bless us all, everyone!" This performance caused Joseph to remark to Vincent, "Now he remembers!" Vincent's referral to little John's failed Tiny Tim performance caused hilarious laughter among the entire family.

As they proceeded up North Broadway, onlookers saw two massive men, one carrying a child and the other with a red headed boy on his shoulders waving to the crowd, twins running ahead, stopping, and then running back, and two women (one carrying a baby) who were engrossed in animated conversation. All were dressed in very fashionable winter garments and all having a wonderful time.

When the entourage reached Phillips Drug Store, across the street from St. Joseph's Church, they paused to enjoy delicious ice cream cones, a surprise treat provided by Nana Carroll. Miraculously, little Mary woke up just in time for an ice-cream and little John curtailed his encore performance (which was beginning to annoy everyone) long enough for a double scoop of vanilla/chocolate. It was after 10 p.m. when the exhausted family arrived home. Within a half-hour, lights were extinguished, and the family was asleep. It was an evening that they would never forget. They would attempt to replicate it for the next ten years.

Saturday, December 23, was a half-day of work for Uncle John and Barney and, when they arrived home around noon, they each had another 22 lb. turkey, compliments of The Shop. Again, Nana and Mom went shopping and the kitchen at Six Moquette Row once again began to fill up with provisions similar to the Thanksgiving preparation of the prior month.

Despite all the hustle-bustle, it surprised the twins that everyone was so happy. They were particularly pleased with *the tips* they received from their paper route customers. They wanted to buy Christmas gifts and were proud that they did not have to ask Mom for money to do it. Even little John had coins that he did not even understand the denomination of. Uncle John had promised and did take the boys shopping later that day.

Talk of Santa's arrival on the following night consumed little Mary and John's daily conversation. "How would he get down an artificial chimney? Where would he put his sleigh? How did Santa know if they were bad or good? Was there an appeal if he thought they were bad and they thought they were good? What could they do with black coal? Was it different than the coal in the basement?" And on and on and on! Joseph and Vincent, who long ago had figured it out, attempted to answer questions but in the end little Mary and John's questions were coming so fast and furiously that they just responded that they didn't know. Uncle John and Barney directed the little one's questions to Nana Carroll, who in turn threatened her sons "within an inch of their lives" if they didn't stop doing it. Mom hid behind the need to attend to little Arthur as an excuse to dodge the little one's interrogations.

Barney came home around 4 p.m., carrying a large Christmas tree that he promptly propped up in the front parlor. The tree was so wide that there wasn't any room to walk around it. Although Nana Carroll's chair was covered with some of its branches, she would not relinquish her favorite spot near the front window and not so gently pushed branches away to make room for her. Rex seemed to take comfort in the presence of the tree and would hide under it for refuge. The first time that he decided to water it, he caused such a commotion that he clearly understood that he must restrain himself in the future after he was promptly exiled to the back-yard.

December 24 was a day of excitement and anticipation as the children awaited the arrival of Santa. At 7 p.m., after dinner, the family gathered around the table while Mom read a poem entitled *A Visit from St. Nicholas (Twas the Night Before Christmas).* When she reached the part where *the stockings were hung by the chimney with care,* Uncle Barney produced stockings for each member of the family. Uncle John cheerfully hung them on the mantle and Mom resumed her reading. The uncles were as excited as the children.

At 8 p.m., the children were put down for a nap because they were all going to Midnight Mass at St. Joseph's. As expected, no one slept because they were all anticipating Santa's arrival. At 10 p.m., true to Nana Carroll's word, the entire family began to dress for church. Like three-year-olds, Uncles Barney and John attempted to make excuses for absenting themselves, but neither Mom nor Nana would hear of it. Uncle John reluctantly agreed to stand in the back, out of eyeshot of Fr. Reed. Barney agreed to stand next to John; that was the most the women could expect of them. At 11 p.m., they began the walk to St. Joseph's Church. The night was unusually warm and clear. The stars glowed brightly above. As the small procession made their way, no words were spoken. They were content to be walking together and at peace with the world.

The pageantry of midnight mass was awesome for the children. The colorful vestments, the religious music sung in Latin by a large choir of nuns, students, and parishioners, the beauty of the decorated church, and the happiness of the attendees, all formed an indelible impression of the magic of Christmas. When the Baby Jesus was placed in the manger, little John vowed that next year he would be a shepherd (it never happened), and that he would volunteer Arthur to be the Baby Jesus (this never happened either). When the mass ended around 1 a.m., the family wound its way in silence back to Six Moquette Row; the children still mesmerized by what they had seen.

By 1:30 a.m. the children were off to bed. Uncles John and Barney warned them that they all had to be sleeping, or Santa would leave without placing any gifts under the tree. Even the generous tray of cookies and large glass of milk that was left at the base of the mantle would not convince him to change his mind if everyone were not sleeping. They were told to get under the covers and not get out of bed for any reason.

The wide-awake children readily agreed but had difficulty falling asleep. The last to sleep at 3 a.m. was little Mary. Barney would check periodically, so he knew who was awake and who wasn't. When he was convinced that they had fallen asleep, he and John began the arduous task of assembling and spreading gifts under the tree. They eventually stopped fighting the tree and placed the gifts in the kitchen area under the table. They vowed that next year's tree would be much smaller.

At 4:30 a.m., Uncles John and Barney finally went to bed. But, at 5:15 a.m., all hell broke loose in the household. Barney was the first to be awakened to screams of "He Came, He Came!! Mom, Nana, Santa was here." Barney could not specifically identify which one of the siblings was doing all of the shouting, because they all were. Uncle John pretended not to hear but when little John and Mary came bursting into to their room and started jumping on their beds, they were difficult to ignore. By 5:30 a.m. Christmas Morning the entire family was assembled in the kitchen. The children were wide awake, and the adults were struggling to maintain consciousness.

From the parlor to the kitchen, the whole first floor looked like the main floor of Knepper's Toy Land. For the children, it was far beyond anything they had ever expected. Prior Christmases yielded one and, at times, two toys per child that they were expected to share. This Christmas was different. Santa had outdone himself. For openers, each boy had his own Flexible Flyer. They would now be able to join the army of sleigh riders who utilized the steep hill of Moquette Row. They would now have their "sleds" to share with the other neighborhood children.

Little Mary's sled would have to wait a couple of years, but her brothers would make sure she had plenty of rides. Next came the bicycles for the twins and the tricycles for little Mary and John; each had a pair of ice-skates. Little Mary had two new dolls to keep Raggedy Anne company, and the twins had a new baseball (leather covered) to replace their taped-up one, and of course, a football. Santa didn't forget Rex either, who was now cuddled up next to a new marrow bone under the tree. Little John had a wooden truck and trains. Mary had a miniature cooking set so that she could work alongside Mom and Nana in the kitchen. Finally, Santa had a new rattle for little Arthur.

And Santa did not forget the adults of the household either. Mom received a new hairbrush and handbag. Santa left a sewing basket and shawl for Nana. Her rocking chair received a new cushion. Barney and John shared a new box of cigars and a large bottle of what Nana called *the spirits*. Each received a shaving kit and two handkerchiefs. All the stockings were stuffed with pencils, candies, little comics, crayons and coloring books.

The bedlam lasted until 10 a.m. when Nana Carroll appeared at the kitchen door dressed in an apron and holding a wooden spoon in her hand. "It's time to prepare Christmas dinner, so we have to clear up this mess," she said. "Boys, take the toys and everything else down to the basement; you can play with them down there. John and Barney, start setting up a table for nineteen people. We can't do much about that tree so move the table further into the kitchen, and we'll just work around it. If you're hungry, oatmeal is on the stove; don't make a mess."

And with that, Mom and Nana began their baking/cooking routine with little Mary underfoot with her new cooking set. When the gifts had been remanded to the basement, the boys bundled up and went outside to try out their new sleds. Uncles John and Barney, who had been working double shifts at The Carpet Shop (to subsidize Santa's good intentions), had hoped to go back to bed, but that just wasn't going to happen. Between carrying and cooking the turkeys, moving furniture, entertaining little Arthur, and sampling little Mary's cooking creations, they were into a full day of household labor. Whenever they began to complain to one another, they were reminded of how empty and childless their home was only a year ago. In seconds, they resigned themselves to an evolving day of chaos.

At 3 p.m., company began to arrive. Uncles John and Barney had already set the table, carved the turkey and placed the various accoutrements around the dining area. Nana had invited six additional family members and a few friends. At 4:30 p.m., Nana called John and Barney into the kitchen and declared that the boys were underfoot and had to be taken outside. As her worn out sons groaned in disbelief John said, "Nana, where in God's name can we take these boys for a half-hour on Christmas Day?"

Mom, who was standing in front of a crowded kitchen counter, moved aside and said, "Perhaps you can get rid of this extra food that is also getting in our way. And while you are doing it, wish Peter Finch and his friends a Merry Christmas."

Spontaneously the two brothers, who were rarely openly affectionate, walked to and embraced both Mom and Nana. No words were spoken, but the look in the sons' eyes said it all. In seconds the uncles, twins, and little John were dressed and out the door, food packages in hand.

"And don't linger," shouted Mary, "we will be eating in an hour."

Anything else that happened that day paled in comparison to what had transpired before. The meal, the greeting of relatives and friends, additional gifts, and a continuation of seasonal greetings fell upon deaf ears. The Sullivan children were on overload. By 9 p.m., the company had gone home, the food and furniture had been put away, Rex was back under the tree and piles of wet clothing were hung to dry in the basement. For the uncles, tomorrow was a work day, and they seemed to relish the thought of a noisy factory to escape to. Their nephews and niece had exhausted them.

For the Carroll/Sullivans, this was indeed, *The Most Wonderful Time of the Year*.

Chapter 4

Serenity Amid Turmoil

✦

1910 to 1920 was a decade in American History like no other. Unparalleled industrial growth and development established America as the leading industrialized nation in the world. The rapidity of change seemed to be the only constant in a world crying out for stability. The Industrial Revolution was propelling society in a direction that even its advocates did not fully understand. In the workplace and home, changes occurred rapidly and often spontaneously, transforming the functionality of society virtually overnight. Some believed the world was in freefall and moving rapidly towards its self-destruction. Most embraced change with a sense of enthusiasm and adventure that more accurately framed the American spirit.

The residents of Six Moquette Road craved the permanence that the society seemed to be rejecting. They had lived through years of uncertainty and had finally found peace and harmony in their blended family. They cried out for a structure in their lives and their surroundings. After years of distress, they were finally in a good place, analogous to passengers who had just survived a very perilous sea voyage. Their ship had reached a safe harbor, and they celebrated their survival and their second chance at life.

For Nana Carroll and Uncles John and Barney, laughter had returned to their home, and they found comfort in knowing that Mary (Mom) and her five children were now safely under their roof. For Mary, the upheaval of the past three years was behind her and life had changed for the better. Her children had a home, and they had father figures in the persons of Uncles John and Barney. Nothing would ever fill the void left by the death of her beloved husband Patrick, but she had returned to her former home and to a loving environment where she and her children could live a normal life.

Since 1886, the Carrolls had enjoyed many happy days at Moquette Row. But the days of the 1911 Christmas season were the happiest. It seemed that every day 0ffered a reason to celebrate and they embraced each moment with a sense of joyful abandonment. Between Christmas and New Years, there was a constant flow of visitors delivering messages of cheer and good will, and, of course, gifts for the five Sullivan children. New companions and neighbors gave each child the opportunity to branch out independently with newly cultivated friendships as they flourished in the security Moquette Row offered them. They now had time in their lives to have fun, friends and comfort in the safety net that Uncles John and Barney provided. When their Christmas tree was finally undressed, and the decorations safely stored, the blended family was exhausted, yet revitalized, as they optimistically faced 1912. Like those fortunate sea passengers, the worst was over.

Birthdays were always a great cause for celebration at The Row. By the time little John, Joseph, and Vincent's birthdays arrived in April, 1912, the family was in a very good place. Nana Carroll was clearly the matriarch whose strong sense of independence established a pattern of consistency that was greatly needed. On this ship, she was the captain. She established the schedule for daily living that set a predictable rhythm for the entire family.

Always the first to arise, she could be heard stoking the stove and preparing the family breakfast, after which she prepared bagged lunches for her boys. Her boys were her two sons, John and Barney, and three grandsons, Joseph, Vincent, and little John. Uncles John and Barney would be the first to join Nana for breakfast. They were followed by Joseph and Vincent, who would guzzle their food, collect their lunches and leave to deliver newspapers on their way to school.

At 6 a.m. the boys were gone, the kitchen was cleaned up, and a pot of oatmeal simmered on the stove. Its maple walnut aroma more than compensated for the smell of anthracite coal that burned all day to keep the house warm. Nana and her neighbor, Mrs. Glenn would then begin their walk to St. Joseph's Church to attend morning mass.

Mom was next to appear. By the time Nana returned from church, little Mary and Arthur were up, fed, and dressed for the day. Dinner was always scheduled for 6:30 p.m. but would fluctuate with John and Barney's work schedule. Nana insisted that the entire family dine together, regardless of the time they assembled. Dinner gave everyone an opportunity to decompress and, in doing so, share the highlights of their day. Saturdays were unscheduled, and the entire family appreciated the opportunity to do their own thing. Sundays would begin with attendance at 9 a.m Mass, a family event that Uncles John and Barney seemed to miss regularly. Dinner was scheduled for 3 p.m. It was the primary meal of the day.

Nana and Mom would spend their day attending to domestic chores, the laundry and house cleaning among them. When the Carrolls and Sullivans left the house, they were always immaculately dressed. Shirts were "starched," and clothing was pressed, and shoes were always shined. Cleanliness was a family priority and bath and showers at the Yonkers Bath House on Vineyard Avenue was on everyone's weekend agenda. Although it was difficult for a family of nine to share the only house bathroom (located in the cellar), somehow they all managed to work it out. The tub and sink were to be cleaned by the most-recent user, and anyone who failed to do so had to deal with Nana Carroll directly. Uncles John and Barney tended to avoid the hassle by visiting the bathhouse at least three times a week.

Clothing was always an important issue for the family, and each child could expect at least one new outfit for Christmas, Easter, back to school, and birthdays. Special occasions, such as First Communion or Holy Confirmation, always called for a clothing overhaul. As long as The Carpet Shop continued to make available opportunities for the brothers to earn extra money, the family would always have ample food and clothing.

In Nana Carroll's later years, her shopping expeditions were greatly curtailed, but her needs were always attended to by Mom, and later, by little Mary. As far as the ladies were concerned, poor appearance was a negative reflection on the entire household, and there would be "hell to pay" for anyone who dared to leave home without being properly groomed and attired. Life for the Carroll/Sullivans was predictable, and in this stability they all found security and comfort.

However, this was not the case outside the home. 1910-1920 was the decade of the American catharsis. It "began with America's efforts to reform itself and ended with its efforts to reform the world (Lone Star College – Kingwood)."

· · · · · ·

America was quickly becoming a highly industrialized country, and with it came all the benefits and ills that accompany rapid growth and development.

While war was raging throughout the world, many social issues were surfacing at home. The advancements of the Progressive Movement (1910 – 1920) were mixed blessings. Prosperity was greatly influencing the changing lifestyle of its citizenry, not necessarily for the better. For every social issue rectified, a new one surfaced as a direct result of that resolution. Some, if left unresolved, would threaten the very fiber of the American way of life. The introduction of an industrial innovation called Mass Production brought many new-social concerns to the forefront.

Mass Production was a major innovation of the Progressive Movement, and it became the new buzzword of the day. Although taken for granted in contemporary society, this was a revolutionary concept in 1912. Mass Production required that moving (assembly) lines be constructed to advance a product being assembled sequentially from one workstation to another where workers waited to complete a specific step in its development. Once a step was completed, the product was advanced to the next station, and so on down the line until it reached the end. At that point, it was finished. Mass Production was a significant labor/cost saving process that changed forever the course of industrial production.

Henry Ford perfected this process, and the introduction of electricity blended perfectly with his methodology. This greatly improved manufacturing speed and efficiency. Under the old system, the Model T Ford built in 1912 took fourteen hours to assemble. However, under the mass production system, it took less than two. The result was that the retail cost of an automobile was lowered, enabling the average consumer to purchase one at the lowered price. As Ford's profits increased, he lowered his retail cost and produced a greater number of automobiles, putting more Americans to work.

The result of Ford's success was a domino effect on manufacturing productivity. Soon other companies in various product fields implemented mass production, resulting in the same cost savings, most of which were passed on to the consumer. Consumer items, once cost prohibitive, became attainable to the average citizen. In the case of The Model T Ford, the $1000 price tag was reduced to less than $400 and eventually to $225 by the end of the decade. Anyone who wanted an automobile could buy one.

Every aspect of life was quickly becoming the end product of a well-conceived assembly line. Canned foods, clothing (once made at home), washing machines, vacuum cleaners, electric ranges, etc., etc., etc., were all now mass-produced. American workers were earning approximately $5 a day. The average annual wage of $750 in 1910 increased to approximately $1250 by 1920. This increase was substantial for the average person who could now purchase the new innovative and labor saving devices.

An increasing international demand for American products drastically reduced unemployment and added to the prosperity of the American family.

Many lived far beyond their means; patriotism was at an all time high. Support for government was confirmed when the sixteenth amendment authorizing a national income tax (on high wage earners) was ratified with minimal opposition on February 3, 1913.

·   ·   ·   ·   ·   ·

But America's new-found wealth had its downside. The clash of cultures caused by new inventions negatively affected many facets of society. For instance, mass production of farm equipment made it more affordable. The result was that crops could be planted and harvested quickly and cheaply, reducing the need for farm workers. Although the need for farm products remained stable, an abundance of supply resulted in lower prices, further reducing gross profits and the ability and need of farmers to hire labor to harvest crops. Displaced farm workers migrated to the cities to find work, and, soon this nation's urban population exceeded its rural.

No less significant was the cultural divide between the traditional woman and her modern counterpart. New devices freed women from performing many mundane tasks that were formally considered their responsibilities. Women now had time to venture into the workplace. Concurrently, industrial expansion created the need for many *white collar workers;* women were now available to fill those needs. Time, availability, changing responsibilities and contemporary expectations created a different woman from what traditionalists were accustomed. The clash between the old and the modern woman was inevitable.

America became further divided on the issue of women's rights when the House of Representatives, on January 12, 1915, rejected a proposal giving women the right to vote. The 15th amendment to the constitution (ratified on February 3, 1870) gave the right to vote to former male slaves and even illiterate white men, but denied this privilege for women, even ones who were educated, affluent, and successful. However, as more women entered the workplace, the notion of "a woman's place being in the home" underwent greater scrutiny, and its wisdom was frequently challenged. Finally, in 1920, fifty years after the passage of the 15th amendment, the 19th Amendment to the Constitution was ratified, giving women the right to vote. Another national crisis was avoided.

Industrialization also spawned other social issues. Labor unions became increasingly concerned about the number of immigrants entering the work force. Conflicts arose between the immigrant and non-immigrant populations. Eventually, the passage of the Immigration Act of 1924 greatly curtailed the number of immigrants allowed into the United States, especially those from Eastern European and Asian countries.

African-American workers migrating to the Midwest and Northeast in search of employment also found themselves in conflict with a resurgence of the highly dreaded Ku Klux Klan, an extremist organization that advocated white supremacy, white nationalism and the end of immigration. Its goal was to reduce competition for available jobs and to stifle this nation's attempt at integration and racial equality.

Humanitarians fought for the adoption of legislation to protect the employee in the work-place. Initially, they fought to ensure employee safety and child welfare; later, they fought for much more. They fought for laws guaranteeing minimum wages, health and safety regulations, and compassion for minors (minimum age and wage laws). The quality of food preparation, as well as the sanitary conditions under which it was produced, all came under scrutiny. Soon labor unions flourished and campaigned for the same concerns.

Demands for regulations establishing mandatory education requirements were frequently at the core of most politicians' agendas. Prior to 1912 less than a third of the nation's children attended elementary school, and less than ten percent ever graduated from high school. By the end of the decade, attendance more than tripled.

But all these issues paled when compared to the discord caused by Prohibition. In 1919, the 18th Amendment to the Constitution was ratified. Often referred to as the Volstead Act, it made the manufacture, import, or sale of alcoholic beverages (such as hard liquor, beer, or wine), illegal. However, failing efforts by the federal government to enforce it in 1920 plunged this country into an internal conflict almost as devastating as the Civil War. The Volstead Act (Prohibition) was extremely unpopular and, as a result, America became fertile ground for organized crime to infiltrate, and it did.

Illegal drinking became something of an American obsession, as even law-abiding citizens drank the forbidden fruit. Good citizens became law breakers. Gangsters, such as Al Capone, Dutch Schultz and Lucky Luciano, became household names. Bribery of police and politicians was common place. Finally, on December 5, 1933 Prohibition was repealed. But the damage it caused to American society was irreversible. Organized crime became permanently embedded in American culture.

While economic growth was measured by corporate ledger sheets, the worth of other important cultural changes was measured by their acceptance into the daily lives of the American citizenry. The advancements in the entertainment industry were enormous. Early in the '20's, talking movies *(talkies)* replaced silent ones, and it was estimated that seventy-five percent of the American public attended the cinema every week. The introduction of Technicolor and the production of elaborate musicals provided an inexpensive form of entertainment for the entire family. Soon, the cinema replaced the live productions that Vaudeville provided.

Likewise, Jazz, whose musical roots resided in the rhythm of African expression, became the craze of the decade. Entertainers, such as Louie Armstrong, Ella Fitzgerald, and Duke Ellington, successfully performed for decades, establishing Jazz as a legitimate art form. Jazz became the popular selection of attendees at music halls in large urban cities like Chicago and New York. This renaissance in music would eventually be accompanied by new dances, such as the Charleston, Lindy, and Foxtrot.

The frustrations of the time found representation in a cluster of authors who rejected post-war values, often referred to as *The Lost Generation*. The writings of authors, such as F. Scott Fitzgerald, Gertrude Stein, Ernest Hemmingway, and D. H. Lawrence, are representative of their convictions.

On the scientific front, medical advances quickly increased the life expectancy of a male, which, in the prior decade, was 48 years to 54 years, and a female from 52 to 56 years; and the future promised even greater advancements.

1910-1920 was a decade when the importance of a stabilized family unit was emphasized, and its individual and collective health warranted greater concern. National prosperity resulted in a reduction of work hours for the average laborer, which translated to more leisure time for the family. Americans utilized this time to pursue various forms of recreation, such as the use of public parks, dance parlors, movie theatres, and the like.

The more affluent Americans adopted ocean cruising as an appropriate pastime activity, but their enthusiasm dampened when the Titanic sank on April 15, 1912. Sports attracted more participants and followers, and organizations for children, such as The Girl Scouts of America, were formed (March 12, 1912). Additional leisure time, accompanied by financial independence, allowed the arts to flourish, and literature that was not normally accessible became readily available to an enthusiastic, growing public interest.

It seemed that in the midst of daily change, very little remained stable. Many restaurants constructed dance floors for patrons to enjoy popular songs and dances throughout the day. The Waltz and Fox Trot were in; the Tango was out. The patriotic songs after America entered World War I, on April 17, 1917, were so popular that singing them frequently led to group *sing-along's* throughout America's establishments.

Musicals drew particular attention from a culture-thirsty populace, and local movie theatres were often constructed to accommodate a variety of entertainments, such as talent shows, vaudeville acts, and touring Broadway productions. Adult entertainment also made its entrance in a big way, and the cry for censorship was heard, loudly and clearly, throughout a religious-based society.

Movies were invented late in the 1800's but, because of the inability of film-makers to coordinate voice and film, they remained silent until the mid-1920. But the lack of sound was compensated for by theatres providing live musicians and verbal commentary to accompany the drama on the screen. Often sheet music was projected onto a large movie screen, and audiences were encouraged to participate in a group sing-a-long.

As filming techniques improved and movies became longer and bolder, they became the center of American contemporary culture. With each new improvement, the public cried for more. By the end of this decade, movie productions numbered several hundred each year and names, such as Charlie Chaplin, Buster Keaton, and Douglas Fairbanks became household words.

The proliferation of some leisure time activities was accepted with mixed blessings. For instance, silent movies provided a major source of entertainment. But some movies boldly brought to center stage the growing social issues of the day. On February 8, 1915, a controversial silent motion picture entitled *Birth of a Nation* made its debut. Originally entitled *The Clansman,* it explored conflicting beliefs as to the role African-Americans should play in America. Its viewing ignited heated discussions and acts of violence throughout the country. The net result of this unrest was that the growing demands of the black community for equality were met with contempt and punitive responses that exacerbated the problem. Movies were becoming the social conscience that many found offensive.

The turmoil and apprehension of this decade were also reflected in the movies and music of the time that ranged from patriotic songs proclaiming American strength and volatility to sadness and despair, as reflected in the Jazz and Blues that filled our theatres and music halls. As America wrestled with its social conscience, sexually provocative movies, music and dances, along with the proliferation of adult entertainment parlors, were countered by cries for censorship.

Technology and prosperity seemed to go hand-and-hand, as an unending stream of new inventions became available at reasonable costs. For instance, the Victrola and the Player Piano added new dimensions to the availability of music to be enjoyed at home. The Victrola enabled families to purchase and play recorded music. The Player Piano enabled a consumer to play piano music either manually or independently via the use of pre-programmed music rolls of perforated paper. As new and more exciting and time conserving inventions entered the market-place, the world looked to America for new directions and innovations.

.   .   .   .   .   .

The City of Yonkers was not immune to the industrial, social, and cultural explosion that had engulfed the nation; in fact, it enthusiastically embraced it. Between 1910 and 1920 its population sky-rocketed to one-hundred thousand plus (an increase of 25% in ten years) as the industrial revolution gathered traction in this ever expanding city. Alexander Smith Carpet Company, Otis Elevator, Waring Hat Co., Bakelite Synthetic Plastics, and many other enterprises expanded to capacity to meet the needs of a thriving and very thirsty nation. Housing and educational facilities also expanded to accommodate the ever increasing needs of a growing city. Likewise, city services, such as the police, fire, and sanitation, grew as social requirements dictated.

It seemed that almost overnight the horse drawn trolleys throughout the city were replaced by self-propelled electric motor cars. One could travel anywhere in the city via the electric trolley. In the summer, the cars were opened and airy for riders to enjoy the summer breezes; in the winter, they were closed to keep the riders warm. The construction of the Yonkers Trolley Barn in 1903 reaffirmed the trolleys' permanency. In fact, trolleys remained in-service until 1953 when they were replaced by newly developing bus lines. Likewise, the automobile, primarily the Model-T Ford (or some variation of same), replaced the horse and buggy and the horse-drawn wagon, as it became more affordable for the average citizen. When the electric light began to replace the gas lamps on major thoroughfares in the late 1890's, Yonkers had truly entered the 20th Century.

Increased leisure time led to expanded leisure time activities, and Yonkersonians proved to be very resourceful. The proliferation of movie theaters such as Proctor's Theater (1914) and the Hamilton Theater (1913) in Getty Square provided movies and live entertainment for several decades, in the case of the former until 1973. Ferry and steamboats graced the Hudson River. Yonkersonians, as spectators, fishermen, swimmers and boaters, flocked to its shores in record numbers. Likewise, the promulgation of city parks and expanded athletic fields added to the growing list of available activities for a prosperous citizenry to enjoy. On a leisurely summer outing, a family could take a ferry from the Yonkers pier across the Hudson River and enjoy a day of recreation in the Palisades Mountains, often picnicking in Alpine Park.

The realization that life had permanently changed in the City of Yonkers came to Six Moquette Row in a very unusual way. At 10 a.m. on April 20, 1914, Mom assigned her daughter little Mary to stand on the front stoop and watch for the Santini Pie and Cake wagon. As had been his pattern, Salvador Santini would prepare a variety of baked goods at his bakery, load them onto his horse-drawn wagon, and travel the neighborhoods in northeast Yonkers, servicing customers.

One of his stops was on Orchard Street at the top of Moquette Row S, where he would vigorously ring a cow bell that signaled to the residents in the area that he had baked goods for sale. Neighbors from all around would descend on his wagon and make their desired purchases. Since this day was going to be a celebration of the twins' and little John's birthdays, Mom stationed little Mary to watch for Salvador so that she could purchase two cakes and a pie for the surprise party.

Mary was almost five years old and incredibly dependable. She was growing up to be a very fine young lady. Already with her tall slim body, hazel eyes and brown hair she had all the features of a striking beauty. When she grew older, she would attract many male suitors. However, with two very large uncles and four brothers, Mom did not think that suitors would present much of a problem for her.

Quiet and soft-spoken, little Mary was a caregiver for her little brother Arthur and a companion to both Nana and Mom. They did not look forward to little Mary starting school in September. But she would start kindergarten at the same time that Joseph and Vincent entered Saunders Trade and Technical High School, and little John entered the fourth grade. Mom's family was growing quicker than she would have liked.

Mom did not hear the Santini cow bell but when she saw the shocked expression on little Mary's face she knew that something strange had happened. As little Mary summoned Mom to the door, she looked out the window to find the pie wagon parked just outside her front door. Why wasn't it at the top of the hill where it normally waits for her? Equally as puzzling, where was Sugar Bell, Salvador's horse? And why did the pie wagon look different? It was "shinny," bright red and green (like it had been freshly painted), much larger than it had been in the past, and enclosed with a serving window and shelf that could be opened to the public. More important, what was the racket that was coming from the front of it, and what was that oil smell?

Mom soon got her answer as Salvador showed off his brand new Lippard-Stewart 4-cylinder Model E Express Truck. It had just been delivered from the Lippard-Stewart Motor Car Company in Buffalo, NY. This day was Salvador's first day of driving it, and he successfully managed to back down the cinder roadbed of Moquette Road S., all the way to the bottom where he stopped just short of the pedestrian stairway. For the next fifteen years, he would make the same descent three times a week.

The inside of Salvador's enclosed truck was lined with shelves upon which he openly displayed his baked goods for the day. As the crowd gathered, more out of curiosity than the need to purchase a pie, he proudly displayed the inside of his truck, his cake shelves, his drop down door that opened to the public, and his 4-cylinder engine. He sadly announced that his horse, Sugar Bell, had been retired to a nice farm in upstate New York after ten faithful years of friendship and service. He told the children that he planned to visit her on weekends and that maybe he would bring her back for a visit from time to time.

Mom eventually pulled Salvador away from his admiring audience to purchase two cakes (one with vanilla and one with chocolate icing) and one apple pie. She teased that his blue bib overalls, green shirt, plaid "bandanna", and straw hat did not fit with his new "riding-machine" image and that he now needed to purchase a full complement of white overalls. Salvador said that they were on back-order.

As Salvador made his way back up the hill, amid heavy exhaust and dense smoke, Mom told Mary that since "tonight was a surprise party for her brothers' birthday," and she could not say a word about Mr. Santini's truck until after the meal and the surprise was sprung. Reluctantly, Mary agreed. But when the meal ended, and the pies and cakes appeared, she did not stop talking about the truck and bragging that she was the first in the whole neighborhood to see it. And when Salvador lifted her up the stairs to see inside, he told her that she was the first person to be lifted inside. As far as little Mary was concerned, this was a very special day. As far as the family was concerned, it was the first time they had seen normally subdued little Mary this excited about anything. It greatly enhanced the birthday celebration.

In June, 1914, Joseph and Vincent were scheduled to graduate from St. Joseph's Grammar School and to attend Saunders Trade and Technical High School. During the past two years, there had been remarkable physical changes in both of them. They no longer looked like book ends, with Joseph growing tall (5'9") and thin and Vincent remaining short (5') and "stocky". Joseph's hair was light auburn while Vincent's was a darker brown, almost black. Both had the intense hazel eyes, which were the family trademark. But whereas Vincent's vision was perfect, Joseph had been wearing prescription glasses for the past four years to correct astigmatism and nearsightedness. Both had masculine good looks, and both attracted more than their fair share of young ladies. Joseph was fun- loving and laid back, Vincent was serious and intense. They were inseparable, and this closeness is what eventually got both of them in trouble.

The twins had been perfectly behaved for as long as anyone could remember. They were both hard workers, good students, and very responsible. Vincent had an almost perfect school average, and Joseph was not far behind. Who would have ever thought they would get into trouble. But, they only had a couple of weeks to go until the end of the school year and, after all, what could Sr. Cecelia do to them anyway? That was their big mistake. They underestimated Sr. Cecelia!

It all started when Vincent discovered glue in a bottle. He was fascinated by what this "liquid stuff" could hold together. Had he not taken a bottle of it to school on that fateful day, there never would have been a problem. But, the entire school was at assembly in the school auditorium when the twins were excused to the boys' room, and Sr. Cecelia's office was empty. In a matter of seconds, Joseph took the glue and told Vincent to stand watch. He, then, proceeded to glue to the surface of her desk every item Sr. Cecelia had on it. Pens, pencils, ruler, two notepads, a daily calendar, scissors, and a desk clock were all fair game as Joseph worked quickly and diligently to do a complete job. When Vincent sounded the alarm that the assembly was ending, they disappeared into the crowd of students leaving the auditorium and returned to their classroom. They had committed the perfect crime; at least, that is what they thought.

Just before dismissal Sr. Cecelia appeared at their classroom door requesting that the twins report to her office. "How did she find out so quickly?" they asked each other as they walked to her office. As it turned out, inquiries made as soon as the prank was discovered revealed that the only children missing from the assembly were the Sullivan twins. They were immediately suspected. To avoid an intense interrogation, they abruptly confessed. As soon as Sr. Cecelia said, "Did you," both boys said "Yes". They failed to give a good response to the question, "Why?" The twins refused to blame one another. They were sticking together.

Sr. Cecelia was amazingly calm when she sent the boys home, directing them to have Mom come to school on the morrow to speak with her. She told the twins that she would not tell Nana Carroll (if she saw her at church) what it was all about because she was giving them both a chance to tell their mother first. Fear left them when they exited her office, and, in a strange way they were thrilled that they had finally done something that would get them into trouble. Their adrenaline was pumping. They knew that some punishment was in order and realized that it would be unavoidable. And then, logical Vincent decided to see what else they could get away with because "there was a limit as to how much punishment they could be given." After all, they were graduating in two weeks. What could they do to us?" On their way home, they planned their next caper.

When they reached home, they told Mom that Sr. Cecelia wanted to see her the next day after school, but they didn't know why. They told gullible little John that they had won a secret prize, and this is exactly what he reported to Mom. School ended at 3 p.m., and Mom's appointment was for 3:30 p.m. The next day the twins told Sr. Cecelia that Mom could not come to school until 4:00 p.m, which was fine with her. Now, as the prank unfolded, the following happened.

Mom was not a small woman and over the past two years gained enough poundage to be considered significantly overweight. As a result, she was having difficulty walking long distances. The twins told her that Sr. Cecelia's office was under repair, and she was working out of the maintenance office until the work was completed. The maintenance office was located in the basement one level below the cafeteria. It could only be accessed by descending an outside staircase that was located in an alley behind the school.

With plenty of time to spare, Mom hiked to St. Joseph's, went behind the school, and descended the long narrow staircase to a locked door at the bottom. On the door was a sign that read;

*I'm sorry for the inconvenience; oil odors have forced me to
move my temporary office to Room 303.*

Sr. Cecelia

It was almost 3:30 p.m., when Mom rushed back up the stairs, entered the first side door of the school and began her ascent to the third floor. Out of breath and extremely tired, she arrived at Room 303, only to find a second note.

*Sorry, I did not realize this room was freshly painted; I had
to move my office to the girls' room on the second floor.*

Sr. Cecelia

Mom was getting suspicious and began looking for answers. She found them on the second floor. Sr. Loretta Vincent was working at her desk in Room 221. Mom told Sr. Loretta about her search for Sr. Cecilia and quickly realized that the twins were up to more mischief. When she finally met Sr. Cecelia in her office at 4:30 p.m., they decided that a serious punishment was in order.

But the twins were not finished yet. When they arrived home, much earlier than Mom, they had concocted another prank. Their initial target was little John, but he was out playing, so they had to settle for little Mary. They filled a large bucket with water and propped it up so that it was balanced on top of the door leading to the pantry closet in the kitchen. Joseph placed the bucket and Vincent prevented it from falling by supporting the part that was hanging over with a four foot broomstick handle. Without the broomstick being held very carefully, the pan of water would tip over, soaking the person beneath it.

Once situated, they called little Mary to the kitchen. By that time Joseph was off the ladder and he pretended that he needed help moving the kitchen table. Vincent said that the table was too heavy for little Mary to move and said that he would help him. He asked little Mary to hold the broomstick while he helped Joseph. Little Mary carefully took hold of the broomstick, and Vincent went to Joseph's assistance. He and Joseph moved the table about two inches and went out to play, leaving little Mary holding the water. She remained in that position for almost an hour until Nana Carroll (who was seventy-four years old at the time) entered the kitchen, realized what had happened, climbed a ladder and removed the bucket from the top of the door. Little Mary was free but very unhappy with her brothers. Her anger was shared by Nana, and eventually, Mom, who was already dealing with her issues.

Dinner table conversation that night was somewhat restrained as the twins were grilled by Mom and Nana with lead questions, such as, "What could have possibly possessed you to do such a terrible thing to Sr. Cecilia?" "Were you trying to kill me?"Asked Mom. "I never climbed so many stairs in my life."

Nana was more concerned about the good name of the family when she stated, "I hope they remember your last name is Sullivan, not Carroll, It makes a difference you know."

"Don't you feel any remorse for any of it," asked Mom.

"Yes," said Joseph, "I wish we had a trick to play on little John."

That was it for the twins. "Not another word," shouted Mom. "I'll get the spoon if I hear another peep out of you. Off to your room where you can stew without dinner. You will not eat with this family again until you apologize too little Mary and me."

As long as they did not have to apologize to Sr. Cecilia, it was ok to show true remorse to Mom and little Mary. They apologized the next morning.

Remaining surprisingly mute during the entire reprimand process were Uncles John and Barney. They told Nana that Mom was doing just fine at handling it. The truth of the matter came out several years later. It was John and Barney who made up the signs the twins posted for Mom to follow.

The next day did not go so well for the twins, either. Sr. Cecilia informed them that, "any further infraction of school rules, or, if you behave in an inappropriate manner in or out of school, you will not graduate and will repeat the eighth grade."

The boys were placed on disciplinary probation and were told that they were inches away from being excommunicated from the church.

"Furthermore," continued Sr. Cecelia, "if you do go through the graduation ceremony you will not receive a diploma. I will keep it in my top drawer, which you obviously forgot to glue, until the beginning of August. However, for the month of July you will report to school every day to help Mr. Fredrick, the custodian." If you miss even one day, or do not work to Mr. Frederick's satisfaction, I will rip it up. Do you understand me? Do you have anything to say?"

Vincent saw the look in Joseph's eyes and feared that he was about to say something he shouldn't. He quickly pulled Joseph out the door saying, "No sister."

Things did not go any easier at home. The twins were punished equally as severely by Mom. They were to report home after working in the school for the month of July to assist with the housework. They were grounded. No sports, no swimming, no biking, no discussion.

For the twins, it was a long, difficult summer. Eventually, they realized that what they did was wrong and were remorseful of giving Mom the *run around* and sticking little Mary with the water bucket. As much as they pleaded for her forgiveness, little Mary remained firm in her feelings of betrayal. But her disappointment did not dissuade her mischievous brothers from future pranks.

By summertime life again began to change at Moquette Row. The twins were back to being their old selves and had earned a reprieve from home punishment. By mid-July, they were free. But not from Sr. Cecelia, who made them serve every minute of every day of their punishment until it was successfully completed. On their last day of work she gave them their diploma's, kissed each one on the cheek, and sent them on their way.

.   .   .   .   .   .

In September little John, who was now in the fourth grade, took over all the paper routes and designated little Mary as his helper. He had completed his First Communion two years ago and was looking forward to receiving Holy Confirmation. He had taken to religion very easily and would, on several occasions, join Nana Carroll for daily Mass if he completed his paper routes on time. The Sisters of Charity recognized him as a possible candidate for the priesthood, and little John had given it serious thought on many occasions. In fact, it was a known fact that if it were not for Mary Maxwell, he would have accepted, in a heartbeat, any invitation to join the clergy. Nonetheless, he maintained his religious commitment, attending mass most days of his life until he died on September 8, 1985. He was eighty years old.

During that summer, the fun-loving twins also came to the realization that they were quickly becoming men and that attending school was an option, as opposed to a mandatory requirement. Their uncles, as well as Nana and Mom, wanted them to get an education, but the choice was theirs. Vincent approached the decision with enthusiasm. He loved school and was determined to succeed. Joseph accepted this decision with the typical laissez-faire attitude that always seemed to get him into trouble. He decided to give it a try.

At the national level, conflicts in Europe were escalating from regional skirmishes to international incidents. War was inevitable.

Little John was saddened with the prospect of going to school for the first time without his older brothers. In the course of the school day, he would always be able to see one or the other and that made him feel safe. Now he assumed the same caretaker responsibilities for little Mary that they had for him. High School proved to be much more time consuming for the twins than elementary school, and they had less time to spend with him. Little Mary had moved into Mom's bedroom, so that was one less bedtime conversation for him to have.

In the next school year students at St. Joseph's Grammar School were still talking about the prank the Sullivan brothers pulled on Sr. Cecelia. The twins had become sub-culture heroes, and little John benefited by being "kin" to them. Little John accepted this mantle with distinction and often laughed with his classmates when they talked about his brothers.

To fill the void that was the direct result of his brothers' growing up, little John threw himself into an active sports regimen, eventually earning the distinction as an outstanding long distance runner on the City of Yonkers' track team. He set long-distance running records that were not broken for twenty years. But his greatest accomplishment was, like his father, Patrick, in baseball. Little John became the finest pitcher in the City of Yonkers. In 1928, he turned down a contract to pitch for the New York Giants, choosing the path of job security with the New York Life Insurance Co., a company he retired from fifty plus years later.

Little Mary thrived at St. Joseph's. She had an unquenchable thirst for knowledge, and her gentle manner made her a favorite among her teachers. She continued to practice her parenting skills on Arthur and would often chat with him for hours about what she learned in school. At two + years old it is doubtful that Arthur understood a word that little Mary said, but that did not dissuade her in the least. Without the Sullivan twins terrorizing the hallways, the 1914 – 1915 school year passed without incident.

Nana, Mom, John and Barney continued to enjoy the accomplishments of the five Sullivan children; what they had become and what they were becoming.

Chapter 5

Bullets, Booze, and Blues

✦

While, at home, Americans flourished in the wealth generated by the Progressive Movement; they were also concerned about the growing escalation of hostilities in Europe. By the early 1910's, talk of war dominated their thoughts and fears.

On this issue, many Americans were conflicted. Their attitude was often determined by immigration status, religious beliefs, social standing, and personal wealth. For instance, because of Ireland's long-standing conflict with England, Irish immigrants and Irish Americans tended to oppose America's involvement; whereas, English immigrants tended to support it. Often decisions and opinions were formed, based solely on ethnicity, as opposed to objectivity. Nonetheless, early in the decade most Americans favored neutrality.

By 1914, most of the major countries of the world were at war, but America still remained neutral. But it was evident that America was sympathetic to the English, to whom it provided weapons, food, and clothing. As the war escalated, America's neutral/non-neutral role angered Germany because its involvement hindered the German war effort. It was inevitable that if America did not reduce its assistance to England, it would be drawn into the war. But the then American President, William Howard Taft (1909-1913), continued to reaffirm America's position of neutrality.

Meanwhile at home, America was also facing escalating hostilities from Mexico. Increased attacks on the citizens of Texas and New Mexico enraged many Americans. By 1916, hostilities had risen to the level where America finally sent 1500 hundred troops over its southern border to capture its primary antagonist, Poncho Villa. As a result of this invasion, secret documents (The Zimmerman Telegram) were uncovered indicating that

Germany had promised Mexico the return of New Mexico and other lands if it would officially declare war on the United States.

This discovery further fueled the cries for war among the American public. It also fueled an unprecedented surge of patriotism. America's war fever was further flamed when Germany stated its intentions to sink all transport ships traveling to England.

On January 11, 1917, Germans sabotaged a munitions plant in what is now Lyndhurst, NJ (The Kingsland Explosion). This attack pushed America to the brink. It was what most considered being the last affront in a number of German atrocities. On April 6, 1917 the United States declared War on Germany. Fortunately, America had been preparing for this decision since 1915 when wealthy and influential politicians launched the Preparedness Movement so that America would be prepared for the inevitable. Funds and manpower were immediately available to a government that no longer vacillated.

The country united around its President, Woodrow Wilson (1913-1921). American factories, coupled with American ingenuity, worked around the clock in support of the war effort. Weapons of war were manufactured at an incredible rate. Planes, tanks, trucks all became the product of assembly lines that functioned non-stop to meet this country's military need.

Patriotism was at an all time high. On May 18, 1917, the Selective Service Act was passed by Congress authorizing the induction of able-bodied men twenty-one years old and older into military service. This Act was later amended to include eighteen-year-olds. When the Treaty of Versailles was signed on June 28, 1919 (it was never ratified by the U.S. Senate), World War I ended and victorious American troops returned home.

.   .   .   .

America continued to lead the world in discovery and industrial development, this time in the area of aeronautics. The feasibility of manned flights took center stage during this decade, as proponents and detractors battled at every level of its advancement. Up to this point the rapid growth of the automotive industry and the incredible advancements in electrical sciences overshadowed man's efforts to fly. However, by 1910 proponents of flight proselytized that conquering the skies was as important to the growth of the American economy as the automobile. Innovative industrialists began to focus on the skies. But the history favored the opponents, not the enthusiasts, asserting that for more than two thousand years countless attempts to fly had failed. But those who believed in its possibility were not dissuaded.

Prior to 1900, aviation progress could be measured by limited hot-air balloon flights and a rare occasion when a plane travelled in distances measured in meters and feet and less than twenty feet above the ground. Balloons were used as spying devices during the American Civil War (1861-65), but governmental or corporate funding for manned flight was minimal. The failures of early attempts were seen as clear indicators of its improbability of success. Flight was an intriguing concept, but, in the bigger picture of what was happening in the world, it failed to capture the imagination of the general public.

Public opinion began to change when on December 17, 1903, in Kitty Hawk, NC, the Wright brothers made the first publicly documented and controlled power-driven flight. Capitalists finally took notice. From that point forward, progress was rapid. By 1912, airplanes were used for scouting missions in European conflicts. In 1914, guns were mounted on airplanes, making them weapons of war. During World War I (1914–1918) airplanes were used extensively. America's interest in flight soared to greater heights by 1918.

Dreams of a man "conquering the skies" rapidly evolved from fantasy to reality when the first intercontinental flight between Scotland and New York was successfully completed in July, 1919. By 1920, talk of flying in balloons, blimps, helicopters, and airplanes became hot topics of conversations. Man finally began to believe in air travel as a viable form of transportation. Aeronautic exploration and expansion became another participant in the mass-production mania.

At war's end in 1919, America joined France, England, and Germany in the competitive peacetime marketing of flight, which had become the new-national craze. The first flight from Scotland to New York made intercontinental air travel a reality. A new American Industry was born.

Throughout the decade, American factories operated at full capacity to manufacture the new inventions that appealed to the interests and pocketbooks of consumers. One who could easily earn additional income to satisfy his insatiable thirst for new gadgets.

·   ·   ·   ·   ·   ·

The City of Yonkers was at the pulse of American Progressivism. Between 1915 and 1920 its population surged by ten percent, as more than one hundred small and large businesses made it its home. As the war movement began to percolate, companies, such as the Alexander Smith Carpet Company and the Waring Hat Company went to the full production of tents, army blankets, hats, and other types of military clothing. Otis Elevator Works, The Federal Sugar Refinery and the National Sugar Refinery contributed greatly in services and donations to the expanding war-effort. Yonkersonians heavily invested in Liberty and War Savings Stamps and War Bonds.

Organizations, such as the Four Minute Men, worked relentlessly to arouse patriotism and to stamp out "sedition and disloyalty to the United States." Throughout the city, efforts to reward and honor men of the military were plentiful. Voluntary organizations, such as the Salvation Army (May, 1865), Junior Red Cross (May 21, 1881), and most church groups, freely "opened their doors" for American service-men. When the War ended, the men who served in the military were welcomed home with opened arms.

Local Home Guard units had been formed to protect people and property if the need arose to do so. Victory Gardens, sometimes called War Gardens, flourished to ease food supply demands and to raise additional funds for the war effort. Likewise, millions of dollars were raised in War Bonds and Stamps. Although there were conflicting views on the merits of entering the war before America declared, doubts dissipated as the fever of patriotism spread throughout the city. The war effort was a unifying factor, as people of all races, colors and creeds came together in support of one common cause. And the residents of Six Moquette Row were in the thick of things.

.   .   .   .

John and Barney Carroll were aggressive patriots. Fortunately, the Sullivan children were growing older and more independent and did not require as much of the uncles' attention as they did in the past. Evening meals and Sunday dinner continued to be a household priority, but the children had formulated friends and interests and no longer saw their uncles as playmates. Their love for the older Carroll brothers had not lessened, though, and continued to be demonstrated in a multitude of ways. However, with the exception of Arthur, the Sullivans were becoming more independent.

By the time America entered World War I, Uncle John was 52 years old, and Uncle Barney was 43. They were both too old for active duty but could serve the war effort at home. They became enthusiastic "fund raisers" and diligent members of the Home Guard, regularly accepting neighborhood patrol duties and vigorously enforcing curfews and governmental regulations. Both were obese, with John approaching 300 lbs. and Barney not much behind. No one was about to disagree with either Carroll when they were enforcing government regulations. With these new responsibilities and an abundance of overtime at The Carpet Shop, the brothers were kept busy. Above all, they continued to feel useful, this time more to their country than to their family.

Nana and Mom became Salvation Army volunteers but as Nana was 78 years old, it was evident that she was slowing down. She could no longer keep pace with the demands of a mobilizing society. She would frequently bake for "fund raisers" and assist in feeding and clothing the less fortunate, but she began to tire easily and frequently "napped," allowing others to assist her. However, once her managerial skills became apparent, the manual labor which she attempted to perform was gradually assigned to others as administrative duties were assigned to her. Many of the workers would prefer to face the Germans than Nana if they missed a duty or failed to complete an assignment. Among the local volunteers, the name Nana Carroll became synonymous with The Kaiser.

Mom (Mary) Sullivan volunteered whenever she could, but with Brothers John and Barney pulling numerous overtime shifts and home watch duties and Nana's involvement with the Salvation Army, more time was required of her at home. At age 40, she still had five children to raise-the oldest, being twins at 17 years of age; followed by John, who just turned 12, Mary, turning 8, and baby Arthur, almost 6. They were wonderful, obedient, fun-loving children who rarely misbehaved. But Mom was not about to neglect them at this very delicate stage in their lives.

The war effort had necessitated a change in the daily morning routine at Moquette Row. With John and Barney's irregular work hours and Nana's Salvation Army duties, she no longer prepared breakfast or lunch for the family. Breakfast and lunch for little Mary, little John, and Arthur were prepared by Vincent and Joseph, who made sure their younger siblings were dressed and prepared for school before they left in the morning. Uncles John and Barney fended for themselves.

Little John and little Mary continued the paper route delivery, and they promised Arthur that he could help when he reached second grade. As a kindergartener, he was just too young. He was barely four foot tall and weighed less than sixty pounds; he was just too small. As soon as John and Mary finished breakfast, they would rush out to deliver papers.

Joseph or Vincent would make sure Arthur was fed and dressed, and the trio would begin their walk to St. Joseph's Grammar School. They would meet John and Mary at the intersection of Vineyard and Ashburton Avenue at 7 a.m., where Arthur then became their responsibility. The twins would then make a mad dash to Saunders Trade and Technical High School to begin their classes. They would have about a mile and a half to travel, so timing was of the essence.

The Sullivans were a close knit family who always protected one another. They seemed to interact without conflict. Their love and trust in one another was limitless. For the older boys, the *rescue walk* of barely six years ago was permanently embedded in their minds. They understood the necessity of sticking together and did so throughout their entire lives.

In September, 1915, Joseph and Vincent started at Saunders. They flourished in this new and stimulating environment. Both developed an immediate interest in the new science of electricity. To them, it was a wonderment that had tremendous potential. Each evening at the dinner table, they would share stories of this incomprehensible phenomenon. Unfortunately, its complexity was lost on their uncles and grandmother. Mom did not completely understand this new science but shared in the excitement her sons seemed to generate.

When electricity reached Moquette Row in the fall of 1916, it was Vincent who explained it to his neighbors and Joseph who helped with the electrical wiring that was snaked through the then existing gas lines to home lamps. It seemed to Mom that every day one or more of the neighbors was asking her sons for help with an electrical appliance or project. Like the proud mother that she was, she freely volunteered them to assist wherever they were needed. Concurrently, as the twins became immersed in this new field of study, they talked of possible business ventures they might explore together after graduation.

As the twins grew older, they grew less dependence on each other. They cultivated separate friends and participated in different after school activities. They still remained each other's best friend, but clearly explored different interests. They even began to look different and by graduation in 1918, it was difficult to identify them as twins. Joseph grew tall to almost 6' and remained slender while Vincent remained at 5'3" with very broad muscular shoulders. Joseph's hair remained auburn, Vincent's dark brown. Joseph remained quiet and reserved; Vincent continued to be outgoing. Joseph was good looking, but Vincent was strikingly handsome. Both remained fiercely loyal to their family and very protective of their siblings. They continued to seek after-school employment so that they could contribute to the financial needs of the family.

Joseph and Vincent never lost their sense of humor or passed up any opportunity to have a good time. But they never seemed to avoid detection when they crossed over the line. A case-on-point occurred in the summer of 1918 when the boys took a break from their lawn-mowing jobs to earn additional money diving for coins in the Hudson River. It was one of those mid-July days that had a little too much heat, but a soothing calm breeze. It was a perfect day for a swim, a bad day for lawn mowing.

During the summer months, a number of large steam-paddle boats sailed up and down the Hudson River from their port in New York City to their farthest destination in Poughkeepsie, NY, a distance of 85 miles. One of these boats was called The Peter Stuyvesant (more commonly called The Dayliner) and it resembled in almost every detail steamboats that were common on the Mississippi River in the mid-eighteen hundreds. Along the way to Poughkeepsie, The Peter Stuyvesant docked to pickup and discharge passengers at Yonkers, Peekskill, Bear Mountain, West Point, and Beacon, NY.

The Carrolls and Sullivans often took day excursions from Yonkers to Beacon, NY, during the summer months to visit with friends and relatives. On a balmy summer day, it was a wonderful way to pass the time, and both Nana and Mom loved the opportunity to sail whenever it presented itself. Passengers often brought accordions and guitars, along with picnic baskets, so that singing and eating was all part of the daily sailing experience.

At each stop, passengers would frequently toss coins into the Hudson from the top deck, and the teenagers at the pier would dive into the river to retrieve them. From the pier, the teens would implore the passengers to throw them coins, and they would normally comply. However, on this day a situation occurred that neither the Carrolls nor Sullivans would ever forget.

Deciding that it was too hot to mow lawns, Joseph and Vincent chose to go swimming, and, perhaps, earn some money diving for coins in the Hudson. They and three of their friends headed for the Yonkers Pier. At just about the same time, The Carpet Shop had a complete power outage and shut down for the day to make repairs. The morning shift, including John and Barney, was sent home. Upon arriving at Moquette Road, Nana Carroll considered the power outage as a good omen and declared that it was a perfect day for an outing on the Peter Stuyvesant. In a moment a picnic basket was packed, little John, little Mary, and Arthur were gathered up, and off they went to the Yonkers Pier with Nana, Mom, and Uncles John and Barney enthusiastically leading the parade.

Meanwhile, the twins and their friends arrived at the pier just as The Peter Stuyvesant had docked. It would remain there for 45 minutes before sailing to points north. However, now at dockside, the teenagers soon discovered that there weren't many passengers aboard and those who weren't about to part with their coins just to see a "bunch of noisy kids jump into the water." As the boys shouted up to the passengers, angry words were exchanged and, finally the Yonkers Pier manager, Warren Grifford, asked the boys to leave. Unhappily, they did so.

Just as The Peter Stuyvesant was about to depart, The Moquette Row gang arrived and boarded it. They didn't know Joseph, Vincent, and friends had just been ejected from the pier. They quickly ascended to the second deck and secured reclining chairs and a prime location at the starboard railing.

As the Peter Stuyvesant departed and traveled a few hundred yards north up the Hudson, little Mary shouted out that her brothers were on top of a hill near a pile of rocks and very close to the shoreline. Mom and Nana at first thought Mary was mistaken, but, as they neared the group of boys, they did indeed see Joseph, Vincent and their usual friends. Obviously, as the five boys waved to the ship and passengers waved back, they did not recognize their family members who had lined the railing to return their greetings.

As the boat passed the boys, they turned their backs on it, dropped their pants, bent over and observed the ship from between their naked legs. They were "mooning" the travelers for not being more generous with their loose change. Mom, Nana, and little Mary were dumbfounded and speechless. Little John and Arthur thought it was the funniest thing and were stopped by Uncles John and Barney when they attempted to "moon" their brothers back. As Uncle Barney's loud booming voice carried across the Hudson, Vincent realized that they had been caught. He alerted the others who quickly picked up their pants and ran away. But the damage had been done. The twins were not looking forward to the evening's dinner.

At dinner, there was little discussion about the ill-fated excursion. Vincent and Joseph were grounded for a month, not permitted to go to the Hudson River for the remainder of the summer, and their friends were banned from the house for an indefinite period. Both uncles thought the prank to be hilarious but wouldn't dare display anything but disappointment and anger in front of Nana or Mom. Little John and Arthur developed a habit of mooning that had a short life-span. On the second occasion, they received a sound spanking and were sent to bed. They never mooned again. Years later, when Vincent returned from World War I military service, Uncle John retold the story to the hilarious laughter of those who had attended his "welcome home" party. Although they desperately tried to control their laughter, Nana and Mom eventually joined the fun.

The twins both signed up for the draft when they turned eighteen on March 23, 1918. Shortly thereafter, they graduated from high school. Vincent was immediately drafted and served the duration of the war, stationed in Virginia as a private in the 31st Division of the NY Volunteers. Poor eyesight and as the oldest son in a fatherless family, Joseph was exempted from military service.

As the now oldest Sullivan attending St. Joseph's Grammar School, little John took his responsibilities to care for his younger sister (Mary) and brother (Arthur) very seriously. Each morning he and Mary would go off to deliver papers while the twins readied Arthur for school. But once they arrived at school, Arthur became John's responsibility. Vincent and Joseph had been very attentive to him when he started school, and he wanted his little sister and brother to have the same sense of safety and security as he had had. He always knew where each was and what each was doing throughout the school day.

At St. Joseph's little John continued to thrive. Like his father, he was an outstanding athlete. He loved all outdoor sports and rarely missed an opportunity to play baseball. He was never very far from a bat, ball, and glove. As a fifth grader, he was the star hitter, pitcher and occasional third baseman of St. Joseph's competitive baseball team. Prior to that time, team membership was limited to eighth graders, but John's skill earned him a place in the starting lineup.

When little John turned thirteen, he played on the City of Yonkers' baseball team, where he earned an outstanding reputation throughout New York State. His 5'4" height and thin frame was very deceiving. Many a competitor fell victim to his slider and fast-ball. His batting average rarely fell below 415. Both uncles took credit for his athletic training and regularly scheduled their days off to attend their nephew's games. As John worked his way through grammar school and his athletic reputation grew, the entire family would attend. Professional baseball seemed a likely career for him to follow despite the discouragement of Nana Carroll and Mom Sullivan, who were concerned about the negative reputation professional ball players had at that time. He had just completed eighth grade when World War I ended.

During his years at St. Joseph's, little John developed a deepening interest in Catholicism. As often as time permitted, he would join Nana Carroll for daily mass. Most believed that he would enter the priesthood when he grew older, but that thought never reached fruition. Like his older brothers, he was enrolled in Saunders upon graduation from St. Joseph's. But, unlike his older brothers, he did not find continuing his formal education appealing. When school resumed in September, he would help Mary and Arthur with the family paper route, escort them to school, attend Mass with Nana Carroll, and then go swimming, fishing, or work at odd jobs along Ashburton Avenue. Meanwhile, his family thought he was attending Saunders.

One day in early September as Nana was about to turn down Moquette Row after walking home from Mass, she remembered that she had an early meeting with Msg. Reid at St. Joseph's Rectory. Mom was on her way to meet some friends on Lake Avenue but decided to accompany Nana back to St. Joseph's and then continue her walk to Lake. As they turned the corner at Ashburton and Orchard Street, they were surprised to meet little John, who was sweeping out Sweeny's Bar and Grill. The deception was over. His truancy had been discovered.

Dinner conversation that evening was somewhat strained as John explained to his uncles, grandmother, and mother that school just wasn't for him. Joseph did his best to convince John of the merits of attending Saunders. Joseph had already landed a good job at Yonkers Electric Power and Light and had attributed the education he received at Saunders as the reason for his successful venture into the employment market. Joseph would continue to work at Yonkers Electric (eventually becoming Westchester Power and Light, and finally, Con Edison) for the next forty-two years. On that evening, Joseph's pleas fell on deaf ears. John was through with formal education.

Nana Carroll was secretly enjoying her grandson's dilemma. She had grown concerned with his near perfect behavior and was delighted when he finally began to rebel. She saw strength and determination in his demeanor that she had not seen before this evening. After all, what was all the fuss about education? The only high school graduates she knew were Vincent and Joseph. Everyone else seemed to do quite well without it. Her silence and soft smile spoke volumes.

Mom was not quite sure how she felt. Her son had deceived her, and that was upsetting. On the other hand, he was almost a man and should be able to decide for himself. She heard his concerns and felt that his voice should be respected. None of her children had ever given her any trouble, and she did not want to overreact to a matter that was not of critical importance to her. As far as she was concerned, John had an elementary school education and that was a lot more than others had had. With Vincent in the army, Joseph at work and Mary and Arthur still in grammar school, she decided to support whatever John wanted.

Uncle John and Barney were indifferent; Uncle John found humor in little John's predicament. Neither uncle had any formal education to speak of and was doing quite well at the Carpet Shop. As long as little John could continue to play baseball, they didn't see a problem. Barney would speak to his foreman (Phil Rothman), and John would speak to the union shop steward (Tommy Fitzgerald). Little John could probably start working in The Shop that week. Mom was greatly relieved to think that her son would be working under the protective eyes of her older brothers and abandoned any objections to John quitting school (although he never attended). The problem appeared to be solved until little John declared that he did not want to work at The Carpet Shop.

The ensuing conversation lasted into the wee hours of the morning, as the uncles attempted to convince John that a career at The Shop was not the worst thing in the world. After all, they had acted as John's surrogate father for most of his life and wanted only the best for him. They could help him further because they were established. They could all be together. Mom felt secure in thinking that her son would be under the watchful and protective eyes of her brothers.

Joseph was never enamored with The Carpet Shop and had vivid memories of the long and tiring hours his uncles had worked over the years and the toll it had taken on their now failing bodies. He felt that John should consider school, reject the carpet shop, and try to find his path. But all agreed that if John did not attend school, he must find a job that offered an opportunity for future career growth.

Finally, Nana Carroll, who had long grown tired of the conversation, offered a compromise. John would determine a reasonable amount of time that he would need to find a job that interested him. If he failed to do so, he would return to Saunders to finish his high school education. If he secured a job, he would become a contributing member of the household. Her demeanor was matter-of-fact and reasonable. John immediately agreed to a three-week search period, at the end of which a final determination would be made. All agreed, and the evening discussion ended on a positive note.

Bright and early the next morning, John left Moquette Row on a quest to find a job. He was fourteen years old. He was certain that he did not want factory work and preferred to be outside in an urban environment.

However, construction did not interest him. He decided to become a corporate messenger. Uncle Barney encouraged him to find employment that offered a sense of permanency and a future. It meant that John would have to look beyond the boundaries of Yonkers.

By the second week, John had expanded his search to New York City. Within three days, he had landed a job as a runner and messenger for the New York Life Insurance Company, located on Madison Avenue in New York City. In 1970, after fifty years of service to the New York Life, he retired as a Senior Insurance Underwriter and Secretary to the Chairman of the Board. Although he never attended high school, he became a self-educated, self-made man by relentlessly taking educational training courses in the field of life insurance. He became a recognized expert in that field. His career evolved from a messenger to an insurance salesman, to a senior underwriter.

As he approached the end of his career, he was resentful of the new requirements that defined high school and at least some college to advance any further than he had. He took great delight in demonstrating that his abilities greatly exceeded those of the college boys, but was unable to secure a promotion to the level of vice-president, a promotion he most definitely deserved. His resentment manifested itself in his absolute insistence that his three children graduate from high school and, in the case of his daughter, Mary, and son, John, college and beyond.

Little Mary was developing into an exceptional young lady, displaying intelligence and poise beyond her years. With her brother John no longer attending St. Joseph's, Mary became the Sullivan family representative and took care of her brother, Arthur. Each morning she and he would have an early breakfast, leave Moquette Row to deliver newspapers, and then attend school. Without ever raising her voice, or nagging, mornings were always off to a perfect start. Her level of maturity, poise, and self-confidence exceeded her age. As she physically matured, her childish little girl looks would give way to stunning beauty. With her grandmother and mother constantly doting over her, four brothers to protect her and her Uncles Barney and John, attending to her every need, she became the center of family life at Moquette Row and flourished with all the attention.

Mary's compassion and generosity clearly identified her as an excellent candidate for a nursing career. As a very young child, she befriended a crippled neighbor (Josephine Sanders) whom she would visit after school and frequently push in her wheelchair to Six Moquette Row. However, her greatest claim to fame was that she was the only one in Moquette Row who could wake Arthur from a sound sleep. Shouting, shaking, pulling out of bed, and other methods all seemed to fail. But somehow Mary always managed to wake Arthur up without conflict. Her secret was one that she never revealed.

As an elementary school student, she excelled. She loved school, and learning came naturally to her. When she assumed the responsibility of caring for Arthur, everyone knew he was in good hands. Mary continued to be Mom's best friend.

As Arthur grew older and bigger, he became a nudge. He always seemed to be into everything and often caused chaos and confusion. For instance, when electric light switches were installed in 1916, Arthur was five years old. He quickly became fascinated by them. He would wander from room to room either turning on or off whatever light he saw. His wooden toy trains were always underfoot, and his insatiable appetite for knowledge resulted in an endless series of questions that adults were exasperated answering. One of Mom's happiest days was when Arthur became a kindergartner.

Throughout the War, Uncles John and Barney worked around the clock in addressing governmental patrol and security issues and overtime shifts at The Shop. They were both exhausted, and it seemed that their fun loving days were behind them. But as the War ended, and an armistice was signed, they were rejuvenated and quickly returned to their carefree ways.

Knowing that Vincent was safely returning home after discharge was a cause for the whole family to rejoice. By the end of 1919, the Carroll/Sullivan families would all be reunited under one roof, and that was a cause for celebration; something that the Sullivans and Carrolls could do in style.

It was after one of these Carroll Brothers' celebratory occasions that a new and noisy component was added to Six Moquette Row. Nana was the first to awaken to the clamor and screams that seemed to be emanating from the main floor kitchen. Among the cries and shrieks was language that was far too *salty* for the children to hear. Whoever this noisy visitor was, he would have to leave. Both Nana and Mom left their bedrooms to investigate the source of the ruckus. When they arrived in the kitchen, they met Uncle John, who was standing in front of a very large, nasty, yet beautiful, parrot who was leashed to a perch that was placed inside a very skimpy wooden cage.

The cuts on John's right hand indicated that his encounters with the parrot did not go well for him. Barney soon emerged to explain that John had won the parrot, whose name was Polly, in an arm wrestling contest at Bronky's Bar the night before. As they discussed Polly in the kitchen, it became evident that the parrot could mimic each speaker and seemed to enjoy the attention.

It was not surprising that Nana and Mom enjoyed Polly. He was hilarious, and John and Barney were finally getting back to normal. Polly would be a perfect replacement for their previously unnamed parrot that died a few years earlier. The issue was what to do with Polly. If he were placed in front of a window, he would make obscene comments to anyone who passed. If he was located in the back kitchen and the doorbell rang, he would invite callers to come inside.

Once while Mom was in the basement, Polly invited Mr. Durante, an insurance salesman, who rang the front doorbell, to come inside. Mr. Durante was confused to have entered a home where he had been invited, but not to face the adult who invited him. When Mom emerged from the basement, she was startled and concluded that he had entered her home without an invitation. As she abruptly escorted him to the door, the poor fellow desperately tried to explain that he had responded to an invitation.

It wasn't until later that evening, as the family was dining, and Polly was chattering away, did Mom realize that the invitation had come from him. For the next decade, Polly became a permanent resident of Moquette Row. Efforts were made to curb his vulgar language, and the family vigorously tried to teach him replacement words. But Polly was irrepressible.

In the mornings, he would mimic Mom calling Arthur to get out of bed from the bottom of the stairs. It ceased to be funny when he began to make his calls at 2 and 3 a.m. He would mimic Uncle Barney calling the new family dog, Fox. As he shouted "here Fox, treat Fox" in his best Barney voice, the poor dog would dash into the kitchen and look desperately for the caller. Polly sat quietly on his perch. When the children grew older, they had to caution house guests about their uncontrollable pet. He was a source of entertainment for the family and eventually, the neighborhood. When Mom brought home a canary to fill the house with pleasant music, it caused bedlam, and the canary had to be returned to the pet store. Polly did not appreciate company or competition. The family could not live with or without him. Eventually, they just accepted him and his irascible nature.

As 1919 drew to a close, it marked the end of a decade of happiness for the Carrolls and Sullivans. What could have become a disaster in 1911, turned into an incredible success story. Words could not describe the compassion and generosity of Nana, Barney, and John Carroll. They rescued a family, and everyone would be forever indebted to them. They were the Sullivan children's surrogate father, protector, provider, and friend. They taught them what a family was, and they did it by example. The family would need the strength they had instilled in them to survive the '20's.

Chapter 6

From Riches to Rags

✦

The incredible industrial growth and accompanying prosperity of the 1910's continued in America into the "The Roaring Twenties" (1920 – 1929). The surging automobile industry was credited with this unparalleled expansion. The latter part of this decade is often referred to as the "The Golden Twenties."

Through Henry Ford's innovative leadership, the automobile industry nurtured many *spin-off* industries, all of which benefited America. By the mid-1920's, there was one automobile in service for every five adults in America. This surge encouraged extensive road construction, the proliferation of gas stations, motels, hotels and, suburban housing construction et al. Inexpensive new cars ($270-$290), along with favorable financing terms catapulted the automobile from being a luxury to being a necessity. For Americans, it meant an abundance of work opportunities in a variety of related fields. Anyone who wanted to earn more money had plenty of opportunities to do so.

When Warren G. Harding was elected President on November 2, 1920, America was recovering from a deep depression, caused in part by the forced transition of its manufacturing industry from wartime to a peacetime economy. Harding pledged to return America to "normalcy" but he died in office on August 2, 1923. His Vice-president, Calvin Coolidge, became this nation's 30th president and in November, 1924, he was re-elected to a full term. By this time, America had returned to experiencing unprecedented financial growth.

During this timeframe, another invention burst onto the consumer market, and this invention would change the world. Italian born Guglielmo Marconi was granted a patent by the United States Patent and Trademark Office for his invention, more commonly referred to as the radio (1907). By 1920, the radio became another wonder of the twentieth century, and the American public's desire to own one exceeded its mass production ability to meet its demand. The radio had arrived, and it immediately became the voice of the past, present, and future. The time communication gap between *happening and knowing* was virtually eliminated. News traveled in minutes, as opposed to days. The world was now communicating in real time.

When Warren G. Harding was elected, it was the first time in history that the new medium of radio was used to announce election results; the world was listening; it knew, immediately, who the new American president was. By 1925, virtually every home in America had at least one radio. Radio had become the primary source of information for the entire world.

.   .   .   .   .   .

When Herbert Hoover was elected president on November 6, 1928, it seemed that there weren't any limitations to the new discoveries that enhanced life and the wealth that an individual could accumulate. But on October 24, 1929, something went horribly wrong. On this day, historically called "Black Thursday," the New York Stock Market crashed, throwing millions of citizens into instant poverty. A decade that promised hope and prosperity ended in devastation and despair.

Black Thursday was the beginning of The Great Depression that impacted the entire western world for more than a decade. The '20's began with a "roar" and ended with desperate cries for help. But help and recovery were a long time away. America did not recover until 1941 when it entered World War II.

.   .   .   .   .   .

The City of Yonkers was a microcosm of what was happening throughout America. Like most cities, it experienced all the benefits and ills of the Roaring Twenties. By the early '20's, it was totally electrified, and its now paved roads were dominated by the presence of the automobile and various other forms of motorized vehicles. Factories, such as The Carpet Shop, Otis Elevator, and the Waring Hat Factory experienced unprecedented growth and prosperity. Workers were earning large sums of money during their normal work day and even more with the availability of overtime. The city continued to be a magnet for immigrants who hoped to participate in the American dream.

Yonkers embraced the Roaring Twenties with a passion for booze, song, and gambling. Like the rest of America, it celebrated its prosperity in numerous illegal drinking palaces (speakeasies) where (despite the restrictions of prohibition) alcohol, good food, and entertainment was plentiful.

Yonkers had its brand of a speakeasy and numerous innovative ways of servicing its thirsty clientele. An underground pipe was constructed that began at The Yonkers Brewery and ended in various speakeasies along its underground route. The tunnels greatly reduced the need to transport alcohol by vehicles, thus reducing the possibility of detection. Nightclub entertainment was plentiful, and Yonkers became the playground for celebrities, the most popular of whom was native born jazz and blues singer, Ella Fitzgerald.

Yonkers Raceway, originally named The Empire City Race Track, was opened for harness racing at the turn of the century and was converted to thoroughbred horseracing in 1907. Throughout the twenties, enthusiastic patrons with sufficient funds filled the stands every day.

By 1923, Yonkers' population, already exceeding 100,000, continued to grow. Jobs were plentiful, and housing was affordable. The terrors of organized crime had not destroyed the city as it had in places like New Orleans and Chicago. Paralleling the population growth was a concomitant growth of the police and fire departments. Public school children were afforded the opportunity to attend an excellent school system.

Parks, museums, movie houses, restaurants, and the like, flourished. The Hudson River became a central recreational area and Larkin Plaza in downtown Yonkers was the center of activity. The stream that once flowed through The Plaza and transported goods from North Yonkers to the Hudson River was covered over to accommodate the parking needs of the riverfront. The Day Liner made regular trips to and from New York City and Poughkeepsie, NY. Trolley service offered affordable and efficient transportation to the waterfront and various other locations throughout the city. Ferries regularly departed from the Yonkers Ferry slip on Alex Street (located north of the Pier) to the Alpine Recreational Park on the New Jersey side of the Hudson River.

Yonkers attracted the rich and famous. Notables, such as William Boyce Thompson of the copper mining industry and self-made millionaires like Samuel Untermeyer, called Yonkers home. As a prosperous city, Yonkers, with its excellent waterfront and proximity to New York City, was an ideal place to live.

.   .   .   .   .   .

January 1, 1920, found the family happy, healthy, and ready to enjoy all the wonders that the future promised. For the blended family, Six Moquette Row was the perfect place to live. Uncles Barney and John were excellent father figures for the children who knew that had it not been for them; the Sullivans would have been destitute after their father, Patrick's death, in 1911. Their love and respect for these two gentle giants was limitless. Uncles Barney and John provided security, stability, joy, humor, and love.

Equally as fulfilling, John and Barney realized that raising their niece, and four nephews had given purpose to their lives. Because of the Carrolls, the five fatherless Sullivan children were given opportunities that many children with fathers did not have. Their uncles were their role models and personal heroes.

Vincent had returned safely from World War I and had found employment in the Westchester Power & Lighting Company (WP&L). He was nineteen years old. His twin brother, Joseph, also worked for WP&L. Vincent's charismatic personality instantly gained him the friendship and respect of his supervisors and fellow employees. His small stature (5'3") made him indispensable when a work assignment required someone to navigate small and confined areas. He liked working with electricity, and he liked manual labor. Each morning he enthusiastically went off to work.

Joseph was surprised one day to meet his twin brother at a worksite, only to learn that they were both employed by the same company. Vincent never told Joseph that he was working for WP&L because he did not want his brother to intervene for him. Joseph had been employed by WP&L for almost two years and had an outstanding reputation. He was recognized as someone with a promising future. Joseph had chosen a career path in management and had just earned the first of many promotions as he began to ascend the corporate ladder.

Vincent, knowing that Joseph would lobby for him, chose to keep his employment in WP&L a secret. Vincent was as ambitious as Joseph but fiercely independent and was determined to make it on his own. Once Vincent's secret was discovered, Joseph respected his brother's wishes, and they went off to work together each day and never discussed the job.

Little John was almost fifteen years old and enjoyed his job as a messenger for the New York Life Insurance Company in New York City. He had rejected the opportunity to attend Saunders Trade and Technical High School but immediately signed up for course work sponsored by the New York Life that would enable him to become a licensed insurance salesman. The life insurance field was the career path he had chosen.

Little Mary was eleven years old and a sixth-grade honor student at St. Joseph's Grammar School. She was continuing the family tradition of being a good student with impeccable manners and flawless grooming. She was growing up to be a beautiful little lady with a personality that made her popular with adults and classmates. The Sisters of Charity saw her as the most-dependable student in the school.

Like her older siblings, Mary watched over her little brother Arthur, who, at age eight, continued to be an irritant. He was in the third grade and was as Sister Loretta often referred to him, "full of life." His superior wit and sense of humor provided the family with many hours of wholesome entertainment and made him very difficult to discipline on those frequent occasions when he went "a little too far."

Mom, at forty-two years old, couldn't be prouder of her children or more grateful to her mother and brothers. Even though brother John was almost fifty-four years old, and brother Barney was forty-five, both acted like five-year-olds, at least as far as Nana was concerned. They loved life and lived it to the fullest. Laughter was part of their daily diet, and they watched over their nephews and niece with the loving eyes of concerned parents. They always attended school functions when the children were involved and were enthusiastic cheerleaders for any who were participating in an athletic completion. Rarely would a young Sullivan look into the bleachers and not see either John, Barney or both cheering him or her on.

Nana Carroll was eighty-two years old and beginning to show signs of her advanced age. Her once rigid figure was now that of an elderly round-shouldered woman who relied upon a cane to support her fragile frame. She weighed a mere eighty-five pounds. She still had her wit and the spryness that had led her family through many a problem. But she was having difficulty walking and quite often slept late in the mornings or napped after attending morning Mass. Instead of stepping, she shuffled along to her destination, rarely accepting the help that was frequently offered to her.

Her walks to church were replaced by rides from one of her sons in the Model T Ford that the family owned. Her efforts to attend 6:30 a.m. Mass often found her attending the 9 a.m. service instead. Her grandson John usually attended the early morning Mass, and Nana loved to go with him. But of late, she just couldn't make it. Nonetheless, when the Roaring Twenties arrived, the blended family was ready to roar with it. But fate had other plans for them.

On Tuesday, January 20, 1920, Barney decided to take a vacation day from The Carpet Shop. Rarely did the Carroll brothers miss work but they had been working long hours for several years and the double shifts during World War I had exhausted them. When the war ended, Barney, as the senior weaver and shop foreman, felt obligated to work alongside his men as The Shop transitioned from producing military products to carpet manufacturing. Now that the transition was complete, Barney needed to rest.

He spent his vacation day doing very different activities. He got up at 5 a.m. and helped Mary and Arthur with their morning paper route. Delivering papers is something he had never done before. When the deliveries were completed, he drove Nana and Mom to church. To everyone's disbelief, he went inside the church with them. He spent the afternoon making household repairs that had been neglected over the years. In the early evening he visited his friend Peter Finch, who seemed to spend his entire life, around a garbage can fire, at the corner of Ridge Avenue and High Street. He returned home in time for dinner and then did something very unusual. He requested that the family join him in a short prayer.

As the family bowed their heads in prayer, they were moved by Barney's softened voice and words that spoke of the love and the appreciation he felt for their lives together. Barney rarely exhibited this level of sentimentality. Dinner lasted long into the night as they shared stories about those special moments that had given them a decade of joy and entertainment.

Nana Carroll was the first to go to bed, and all but her sons, Barney and John, soon followed her. As they bid each other goodnight, Barney responded in his usual, "See you in the morning." John and Barney talked into the early morning about their good fortune and the pride they shared in raising the children. Both had to work the morning shift and finally went to bed sometime after midnight.

Early that morning Uncle Barney died in his sleep. When John was unable to awaken him at 4 a.m., he alerted the household and sent Joseph to summon Dr. Lee. But it was too late. The gentle giant of Moquette Row had passed on June 21, 1920, at 6:40 a.m. The cause of death was determined to be a heart attack, technically the dilation of his heart.

Uncle Barney's death was the first the family had faced since Patrick Sullivan, Sr., died in August, 1911; and, like Patrick's death, Barney's was also unexpected. He was rarely ill and never complained of any health-related problems other than indigestion. As his lifeless body laid at rest in the parlor of Moquette Row, memories of Patrick, Sr.'s, wake were painfully recalled by all of the family except Mary (who was an infant at the time) and Arthur (who was not born). Uncle Barney's death was devastating.

Nana sat silently beside the lifeless body of her son for the three days he laid at rest. She was the last to leave him in the evening and the first to sit with him in the morning. The entire family maintained a daily vigil as hundreds came to mourn the passing of a trusted neighbor and friend. Arthur had the most difficulty accepting his uncle's death because he could not understand why God had taken him, and, if he was with God, why was he sleeping on a block of ice on a platform in the parlor, and why couldn't he wake him up? His frequent questions to anyone who would listen elicited a response of "I'll tell you later." But Arthur never received a satisfactory answer. He eventually stopped asking.

A home that was filled with laughter was now one of sadness and tears. As the horse-drawn carriage slowly carried Barney's body from Moquette Row to St. Joseph's Church for a Requiem Mass, the family quietly walked behind it. Nana Carroll insisted on walking behind Barney's casket from The Row to the church. She struggled with each step but would not accept any assistance except her son, John, who virtually carried her with his powerful right arm. Hundreds of mourners silently walked down Orchard Street and up Ashburton Avenue behind her. The trip from St. Joseph's Church to St. Joseph's Cemetery was completed by automobile and hearse. From that day forward, Nana Carroll dressed in black like her daughter, Mary, who had worn black since her husband, Patrick's, death in 1911.

Life after Barney was painful for the family. Nana Carroll was more withdrawn, and the family feared that she would not recover. John Carroll, once the vociferous uncle, clearly had lost that spark that triggered his incredible sense of humor. He no longer played practical jokes and seemed to be disinterested in playing ball with little Arthur, something that he and Barney loved to do. But John was now sixty-five years old, and most rationalized that given his enormous size, slowing down was just part of the natural process.

Mom and Barney were three years apart in age and, thus, they grew up together. They were confidants and best friends. Her loss was profound. But Mom knew that her children were also grieving and that she must maintain strength and optimism for their sake. She believed that with the passage of time the family would normalize and by New Year's Day (1921) that appeared to be happening.

As the twins' twenty-first birthdays approached (April 27), Nana, Mom, and Uncle John decided to continue with their long time plans to have a birthday party. The celebration was Uncle Barney's idea and he, and his brother, John, had spoken about it on many occasions. They wanted to do something special as each of the Sullivan's reached the age of twenty-one. They saw this age as a symbolic fulfillment of the promise they made to Mom in

1911, i.e., to care for her children until they reached adulthood. Not to follow through would have been disrespectful to Barney's memory, so they moved forward with the party as planned.

The April 27 birthday gathering at Moquette Row was intimate and mellow. Barney's absence was felt as they tried to celebrate this milestone. Nana Carroll and Mom prepared a birthday cake. The evening ended early but not on a somber note. The twins enjoyed it and appreciated the courageous efforts of the family. There was no doubt in their minds that this was what Barney wanted, and they took solace in knowing that they were honoring his memory.

By May, 1921, laughter was slowly returning to Moquette Row. The family had turned a big emotional corner. Other than Nana, Barney's death seemed to have affected Arthur the most. The rest of the family attempted to help him cope by giving him more attention and greater understanding when he misbehaved. Over the years, Arthur had attached himself to both Barney and John, and they felt a real connection with him because he was barely three months old when he moved into Moquette Row. The uncles saw Arthur as their son, and he saw them as fathers. He was born two weeks after his father's death (Patrick Sullivan) so he never had any connection with him. Uncles Barney and John were the only adult male figures he knew.

Although it had been less than a year since Barney's death, the family attempted to engage Arthur in activities that he enjoyed as a distraction from his preoccupation with thoughts of Uncle Barney. It was on just such an occasion that a tragedy struck again.

On May 23, 1921, Mom Sullivan did something very unusual. She allowed Arthur to miss a half-day of school so that she could take him to the movies to see a series of new cartoons that were being shown at a matinee show at The Terrace Theatre (The Itch), located just a few blocks from the Moquette Row home. When Arthur heard that he was going to the movies with Mom, he was ecstatic. This outing would be the first real entertainment he had had since Uncle Barney had died. Going to the movies was one of Arthur's favorite things to do. The entire family vicariously enjoyed Arthur's happiness as he excitedly waited for movie day to arrive.

Mom and Arthur were among the first to arrive at The Terrace and had their choice of seats; for Arthur it was the first-row-center. At 1 p.m., the house lights dimmed and the crowded theatre became silent. The show was about to begin. But, shortly after the first newsreel the theatre's matron, Mrs. Clooney, directed that the house lights be turned up. Over the loud boos of a large audience who was upset by her interference with the movie, she loudly asked if there was a Mary Sullivan present. There was a hush over the crowd as Mom immediately identified herself. Mrs. Clooney very solemnly asked her to report to the manager in the lobby. When she arrived, she met her son Joseph, who was visibly distraught. She knew something was wrong.

Before he could speak any coherent words, Joseph broke down into uncontrollable sobbing. From the background advanced Uncle John, who delivered the message that Joseph could not. The unthinkable had happened. There had been a terrible accident at work. Her son, Vincent, had come into contact with live electrical wires and was immediately consumed in flames. He was rushed to New Rochelle Hospital, but the prognosis for survival was not good. Immediately the family rushed to Vincent's bedside but it was too late. Vincent had died of shock and burns. He had just turned twenty-one years old.

The news to the family was crushing. They had not yet recovered from Barney's death and now must face Vincent's. He was so young and vibrant that it was incomprehensible that he was dead. His body was burnt beyond recognition, and so it was placed in a closed casket. For three days, he laid at rest in the parlor at Six Moquette Row as a broken family attempted to cope again with a death. Just barely sleeping, Nana, Mom and Uncle John maintained a vigil around the clock. As more than a thousand well-wishers passed by the casket, words of sympathy were exchanged regarding the extraordinary nature of the man and the senselessness of his death. Vincent had escaped the perils of war, only to return home to die. It was impossible to accept. How could something like this happen?

Nana said very little and spent most of her time consoling Uncle John, who would break down and sob uncontrollably whenever he engaged in dialogue with anyone. He was almost sixty-six years old, significantly overweight, and his body, which had been engaged in hard manual labor for fifty-five years, was worn out. The family was concerned and rightfully so.

As little Mary, who was now eleven years old, sat beside the coffin of her brother, she remembered the little boy who held her hand so tightly through a snowstorm to bring her safely to Moquette Row ten years earlier. Vincent was her protector and friend. He knew her secrets and knew her dreams. He was the person who helped her sort out the complexities of life. She felt isolated and alone.

Little John would soon be sixteen years old and was difficult to read. He was quiet and showed little emotion. His love for his brother, Vincent, was unquestioned, but his lack of an emotional display was baffling. For the remainder of his life, he would deal with tragedies, deaths, and crises in the same stoic way. He internalized his pain and suffered quietly and privately.

Nana was overwhelmed. Vincent was a "free spirit" that held the household together. His compassion and his wit helped carry the family past the death of Barney and his comforting smile always conveyed the message that "things were going to be ok." He was never too busy to help and never required anything other than a meal, room, and a friendly smile. He was the consummate family man and was destined to be an incredible husband and father. He had been Mary's unofficial guardian most of her life. He was the talkative one; the one who was always open with his thoughts and hopes. He was a planner, and he was a dreamer. To everyone who knew him, he was extraordinary.

For Joseph, the death of his twin brother was unbearable. Vincent and he were best friends, and their loyalty to each other was unshakable. They shared in each other's successes and suffered equally when one or the other had failed. The competition between them was non-confrontational. Joseph was always the better athlete and the taller of the two. However, he would never consider running up the score in a one-on-one basketball game or play too aggressively in a football game. Joseph would always do just enough to win, but nothing more.

On the other hand, Vincent was a "people person" who was outstanding at building personal relationships. He was handsome, outgoing, and articulate. But he would never exclude his brother from a conversation, disagree publicly with him, or prevent him from participating in any activity that could be shared. Their individual personalities blended in an incredibly harmonious way. The result was the emergence of a third personality that incorporated the existing two. And when it came time for decisions to be made, they acted in one voice.

As Joseph sat beside the coffin of his brother, he thought about their recent conversation and the secret that they shared. For a long time, Joseph had dated a young woman named Mary Phillips. Mary was articulate, independent, beautiful, and confident. She was a perfect complement to Joseph and met with Vincent's unconditional approval. Joseph and Mary were secretly engaged and planned to marry that June (1921). Vincent was going to be Joseph's best man, and together, they agreed that the family should be told on June 1st. The couple wanted a private ceremony and, in light of the recent deaths of Mary's (Phillips) brother, Willie, and sister, Kathryn, coupled with the death of Uncle Barney, they believed that a large celebration would be inappropriate.

Now, along with attempting to cope with the death of Vincent, Joseph was now struggling with the decision regarding his marital plans. His facial expressions and sunken body posture projected a man in agony. He did not know what to do and had no one to turn to. He had lost his confidant and best friend.

One month later Mary Phillips and Joseph Sullivan secretly married in a private ceremony at Our Lady of Mt. Carmel Roman Catholic Church in Yonkers, on June 16, 1921. Although they did not intend to announce their marriage until better times prevailed, their secret was discovered when Mary Phillip's mother, Mary Finnigan, found their hidden marriage license among her daughter's personal belongings. Shortly thereafter, the Phillips held a small festive celebration and Joseph moved out of Six Moquette Row to join his new bride.

In later years, the newlyweds defined their secret marriage as an act of love. They both had recently lost loved ones and had turned to each other for comfort and support. They realized that the recent series of tragedies impacting both families (four deaths within two years) would mean that their wedding would have to be postponed for an indefinite period. They feared that if another tragedy struck, they might never marry.

There was no ideal time for them to wed, so they decided to marry in secret and wait until a more opportune moment to tell their families. An accidental discovery was that "more opportune moment" and they were relieved when both families accepted their wedding with happiness and a genuine attempt to celebrate.

As Mom Sullivan observed the behavior of Nana, Uncle John, and her now four surviving children, she realized that she had to be the standard bearer who held the family together. Nana and Uncle John were no longer emotionally capable, and little John, little Mary, and Arthur were too young. Joseph was now married and must build a life with his new wife. The family needed her wisdom and her strength. She knew that her grieving must be done in private. Depression could destroy their will to live. Mom could not let that happen. She was now the matriarch.

.   .   .   .   .   .

As a young woman, Mom was fiercely independent. She married Patrick Sullivan, despite the very aggressive opposition of his family. When Patrick died, she was destitute but determined to carry on with her five children. When her brothers invited her and her children to live with them at Six Moquette Row, she first declined. Repeatedly they asked and repeatedly she refused. Finally, she relented, believing that her brothers were determined to take her and her family home with them, by force if necessary. Had she continued to resist, that is exactly what they had intended to do.

When her brothers insisted that she stayed home to care for her children; she again resisted, but, once again their determination and undeniable logic prevailed. After much consternation, an agreement was made. Uncles Barney and John would financially support the family, and Mom would care for her children. But with Barney's and Vincent's deaths, former agreements crumbled. Uncle John's emotional collapse and Nana's failing health clearly defined Mom's role. She was now the decision-maker, and the future of her family depended on her to lead them.

With the tragedy of Uncle Barney's and Vincent's deaths behind them, the remaining family picked up the pieces of their emotionally shattered lives and attempted to move on. Immediately following Vincent's interment in St. Joseph's Cemetery in Yonkers, NY, Uncle John retired from The Carpet Shop and spent most of his time moping around Moquette Row. He was a lost soul who openly admitted that the absence of Barney working beside him at The Shop and the tragic death of Vincent were beyond his ability to cope. When Joseph moved out to join his new wife in the fall of 1921, he was devastated.

However, when life seems to be at its lowest point, something good usually happens; and, in this case, a newborn named Joseph Sullivan, Jr. (later to be called Junior), entered the picture. On July 13, 1922, Joseph presented his first-born son to the family. Good news provided good reason to celebrate. Little John became Junior's godfather, an honor he cherished for his entire life. Mom treasured her first grandchild, second only to Nana Carroll, who was beside herself with happiness. After years of being depressed, she seemed to come alive again. She became a proud and very verbal great-grandmother who anxiously wanted to care for a newborn. Junior was the rallying point the family so desperately needed.

Shortly after Junior's birth, the Joseph Sullivans moved back into Six Moquette Row to help Mary Phillips Sullivan recuperate from her difficult pregnancy and to allow Joseph time to find larger living quarters. But their stay was brief. One evening while Nana Carroll was diapering Junior, she picked him up by his heels and made the sign of the cross with his body; his head was swinging several inches above the table. But despite her good intentions, she was fragile, and the possibility of her dropping Junior was very real. Making the sign of the cross with a baby's body was a common practice among the Irish of that time.

When a shocked Mary Phillips Sullivan questioned Nana about the risk to Junior's safety, Nana proclaimed that this was the way she diapered all of her children and grandchildren, and this is the way she intended to diaper her great-grandson. The fate of the Joseph Sullivan family was sealed. Joseph accelerated his efforts to find suitable living quarters and did so shortly thereafter.

Three reasons compelled Joseph to move his family out of Moquette Row- the obvious need for privacy being one, the overwhelming presence of the memory of Vincent being another. The third, but equally as compelling, was based in Irish folk-lore. The Irish of the time were a very superstitious lot, many of whom believed that tragedies happen in clusters of three. The elderly often kept track of tragedies. On the second of a similar occasion, such as death, they would wait in anticipation of the third. Within a period of eleven months, Barney and Vincent had died. Privately, many of the predominately Irish neighbors questioned "who would be the third?"

Mary Phillips Sullivan did not wish to tempt fate and was determined that her son, Junior, was not going to be that fatal number three. Although she and Joseph would deny placing any stock in this superstition, they were not taking any chances. By August, they had relocated to a small apartment in North Yonkers. However, as it soon would be discovered, Junior Sullivan was not yet on the Grim Reaper's list; Nana Carroll was.

As best as her physician, Dr. Lee, could determine, Nana had contracted either scarlet fever or strep throat sometime during 1910. With limited medical remedies available, this infection lingered in her body for more than a decade. Historically, this was around the time when her family was in turmoil because of Patrick Sullivan's death (Mom's husband), immediately followed by the birth of Arthur (Patrick), Mom's fifth child.

Nana rarely sought medical attention but during that time she would have been less inclined to do so. She would have assumed that any discomfort she experienced would have been caused by stress as opposed to sickness. She would have kept her discomfort to herself, not to create any further difficulties for her children. And she didn't have much use for the medical profession.

The result was that Nana had become noticeably ill in June 1920, coincidentally around the time of her son Bernard's death. Her physical discomfort was obvious, and the remaining family members insisted that she sought medical attention. Shortly thereafter, Dr. Lee diagnosed her condition as Chronic Nephritis, more commonly referred to as kidney disease. This condition was linked to her prior illness and was incurable.

Over the next two years, Nana's health worsened. Frequently she would become disorientated, and at times, she would lose her balance and stumble or fall. She required a great deal of help and was forced to swallow her Irish pride and accept assistance from her family to perform the most common of tasks, such as walking or dressing. Although she never lost her sense of humor, she would often become disoriented, losing track of time and conversation.

Each morning her son, John, would carry her down the stairs from her bedroom to the parlor. There, she would remain in her overstuffed chair for the entire day, being attended to by Mom, or her granddaughter, Mary. If she were in pain, she would never admit it, but there was little doubt that her memory was deteriorating, and she had lost her will to live. Her body was shutting down. Often in the early evening John would carry her to bed where Mom and Mary would change her into her sleeping garments, even as Nana slept

On January 13, 1923, Dr. Lee was again summoned to Six Moquette Row. At the end of his examination, he concluded that Nana's kidney disease had developed into Uremia and that her body was retaining fluids faster than it could expel them. Her condition had changed from critical to terminal. It was simply a matter of time. On Dr. Lee's last visit on January 24th, he notified the family that the end was near.

Throughout the night, they remained by her bedside, hoping beyond hope that her comatose body would rally one last time. But at 10:43 a.m. on January 25, 1923, Nana Carroll died. In her final days, she would drift into frequently inaudible conversations with her deceased son, Barney, or grandson, Vincent. Perhaps in her mind, she was rushing to greet them; or, they were coming to take her home.

For the third time in less than three years, the remaining members of the blended family assembled in the parlor at Six Moquette Row to bid farewell to their matriarch. A few friends and neighbors visited but for the three-day-vigil the attendees were primarily the grief stricken family. They sat silently, rarely speaking to sympathizers or each other. What could anyone say to ease the pain of a close family who had endured so much together? They heard all the words and knew that Nana was at peace. But somehow, those words were no longer consoling. Death had numbed them. Nanas past three years had been filled with sadness and pain. Her body was shutting down, and, mentally, she was confused. Despite the efforts of a caring and attentive family, Nana's quality of life had worsened.

The family did find comfort in knowing that she was no longer suffering. They believed she was reunited with her beloved husband, Bernard (who passed in 1884), her son, Barney, and her grandson, Vincent; and that thought was consoling. Perhaps when she was overheard speaking to them the night before she died, she was telling them to expect her. Now, she was comfortably in their embrace.

With the passing of Nana, Six Moquette Row became a very different place. Absent were her wit and her cheerful, comforting manner. The narrow rooms that were once filled with laughter were now silenced by death. The family was floundering. Mom and Uncle John had grown up at Six Moquette Row. To them, the voices of Nana, and Barney were always present. The loss of life over the past three years was devastating.

A month after Nana's death, Uncle John retired from The Shop and left The Row for parts unknown. He found it too difficult to cope with the loss of Barney, Vincent, and Nana. The depth of his depression worried the entire family. He was grief stricken, and he needed to find his way to survive. He needed privacy to deal with his emotions that were drifting out of control. He was haunted by the memories of Moquette Row and saddened by what was no longer there. For the next five years, he would periodically wander off, only to return again to The Row. Sometime during this period he married Elizabeth Malone; a woman who was unknown to the family. Elizabeth died prior to 1930. Life for Uncle John had become tragic. Early in 1931, he returned to live at The Row for the last time.

Uncle John's childlike personality did resurface from time to time, especially when he played Dominos with his grand-niece, Gloria, Joseph's second child, who was born on December 28, 1923. As they grew older, she and her brother, Junior, played a sustaining role in Uncle John's life.

When Uncle John's nephew, little John, married Mary (Mae) Maxwell, the little girl from across the street on June 26, 1928, he loudly boasted that he knew it would happen. Little John and Mae's courtship had been a long one (from age 7 to age 23), complicated by the fact that Little John was a devout Catholic and Mae was raised a Protestant. If religious differences were not enough of a problem, Mae was born in Scotland and thus was not a United States citizen. But love prevailed and in 1959, after thirty-one years of a happy marriage, Mae converted to Catholicism and became an American citizen in the same year. Little John insisted that he did not play any part in Mae's decisions. Those who knew them well believed that to be true.

Uncle John died peacefully at Six Moquette Row of heart disease at 8 a.m. on September 8, 1937.

All that now remained of the blended family at Six Moquette Row was Mom, little John, little Mary, and Arthur. One morning Mom removed her rocking chair from the parlor and sat in the overstuffed chair that was once Nana's. From that moment on, for the next twenty-nine years, that chair was Mom's place by the front window. As she observed the neighborhood that had been her home most of her life, she thought about the family members who had died. She also reaffirmed her intentions to live for the sake of the remaining blended family members.

When Nana died, Arthur was twelve years old and in the sixth grade. The paper route that was once the job of brothers Vincent, Joseph, and John was now his sole responsibility. And each morning he would faithfully perform those duties alone. Later in the morning as he wandered the halls of St. Joseph's Grammar School he missed seeing his brother John and sister Mary. He was the last Sullivan of that generation that would attend and the thought of it made him sad.

Mary was fourteen years old and attended Sacred Heart High School in North Yonkers when Nana died. She was pursuing a career as a secretary and continued to earn outstanding grades and evaluations. When she took a job as a bank teller in the Empire State Building, in New York City, upon graduation in 1927, she was very successful. So successful, in fact, that when she turned twenty-one years old, she secured the position of head teller at The Central National Bank (CNB) in Yonkers.

Mary's move to CNB was due, in part, to her marriage to Thomas Baldwin, who was also employed in the same bank at the Empire State Building. Bank policy prohibited married couples from working together, so either Mary or Tommy had to change jobs. To Mary's credit, she made the move, and her expertise was immediately recognized. A promotion from teller to head-teller was imminent. A managerial assignment was a significant position for a woman of her young age to hold. Her future was very promising.

Mary became Mrs. Thomas Baldwin in May of 1937. Regrettably, her lifeline was not an extended one. She died of cervical cancer on July 5, 1950, at the age of 41. She was survived by her son, Joseph Baldwin, who was born on August 30. 1939. Joseph continued to live with Mom Sullivan at Six Moquette Row.

The youngest of the blended family, Patrick Arthur Sullivan, also died tragically. He attended Cathedral High School in New York City, graduating in 1929. He married Rose Marsh around 1938, and they had a daughter who died shortly after birth. Arthur became an extremely skilled bookkeeper for the management company of Grand Central Station in New York City. After suffering for several years with an undetected brain tumor, he died on the operating table on August 20, 1940. He was twenty-nine years old. Now only three members of the blended family survived him, Mom, Joseph and little John.

· · · · · ·

As the branches of the next generation's tree began to bloom. Mary Phillips Sullivan and Joseph added two additions to their family of four when their second son, Roland, was born on April 3, 1929, and their second daughter, Janice, was born on June 7, 1931.

Mary (Mae) Maxwell Sullivan and (Little) John Sullivan added three more additions to the tree when daughters Mary (June 27, 1931) and Patricia (May 23, 1934), were born, followed by a son, John, on March 29, 1942.

Completing the circle of the blended family, Mom Sullivan died on April 25, 1952, at the age of seventy-five, once again another victim of heart disease. Her son, Joseph, died at age sixty of a heart attack on January 31, 1961. And her son, John, was the last to die on September 8, 1985. He also died of heart disease.

Six Moquette Row was sold shortly after Mom's death in June 1952. On that day, little John, now 47 years old, sat alone on its front stoop and wept.

Joe Baldwin went to live with his godfather, Joseph, Mary Baldwin's brother.

In 1954, The Alexander Smith Carpet Company closed, displacing many Yonkers families.

In 1974, as part of a project to widen Nepperhan Avenue, Six Moquette Row, along with several other row houses, was demolished by the City of Yonkers.

· · · · · ·

One can only imagine the grief Mom, Joseph, and little John suffered in the latter years of their lives. They had witnessed the deaths of all the others who had joined them at Six Moquette Row on that cold, winter evening on November 11, 1911.

In little John's case, as the last to die, he must have had times when he felt very alone, although his stoic personality would never allow him to verbalize it. In his later years, he would often call out to one of the blended family in his sleep. He never spoke of his father's side of the family. To him, Denis and Sarah Sullivan never existed. He remembered his father, Patrick, but it was a vague memory because he was six years old when he died. The most he would say about his father was "that he must have been a wonderful person because if he weren't, Mom would never have married him."

All of the children had vivid memories of *The Rescue* and considered Uncles Barney and John to be their dual fathers. Whenever they spoke of them to their children and grandchildren, they spoke with reverence, respect, and love. The blended nine were their world at a crucial time in their lives.

.   .   .   .   .   .

Although this story ends with the death of little John in September, 1985, it is, for future generations, a starting point for the next family member to come forward and continue to expand upon the story of this incredible family. From the marriage of Patrick and Mom, in 1894 to the present time there are more than eighty descendants. The bloodline of Patrick Sullivan continues and is patiently awaiting the next family member to carry on where this story leaves off.

In the history of this family, there were many giants. Because of age and time, the most remembered by her grandchildren was Mom Sullivan. The majority of the blended family had died before her grandchildren were born. For them, Mom emerges as a true heroine.

To her grand-children, Mom represented unconditional love and perfection. She never spoke of the loneliness and pain she silently endured. At a time when strong, determined women were not fashionable, Mom Sullivan was an inspiration to anyone facing difficult times. She lived through the deaths of her parents, brothers and sisters, and three of her five children. She never complained and never gave up on life or faltered in her faith. Among this generation of strong, courageous people, she was the standard bearer.

Her grandchildren hope that in some small way, this story serves to preserve the memories of Mary Carroll Sullivan (Mom) and Uncles Barney and John Carroll. They were models of love, strength, family devotion, and loyalty to each other and to their faith. They are the heroes—*"the wind beneath our wings."*

Afterword

For the next ancestor of the blended family who would like to continue with this storyline the following is offered:

Denis Sullivan, Sr., was born on January 15, 1843 in County Cork, Ireland. His father's name was John Sullivan, his mother was Mary Driscoll. No other information regarding his parents is available at this time.

Sometime during the mid-1850's Denis married Ellen Cronin in Ireland. Prior to migrating to America in 1863, he fathered three children:

John (1861)　　　Mary (1861 ?),　　　James (1864).

He then migrated to America in 1863 and was joined by his wife and three children around 1868. Ellen Cronin died in the childbirth of her daughter, Cathrine.

Cathrine 9/ 25/1869.

Denis remarried Sarah Duffy (also an Irish immigrant) on November 10, 1870. In this marriage, he fathered nine (9) children.

Margaret (9/11/1871),　　　Kathryn (Kit)(5/30/1874),　Patrick (4/3/1876),
Sara Lilian (Lil) (9/271877),　Thomas (6/1/1879),　　　Denis (4/17/1881),
Mary Agnes (8/28/1882),　Peter (11/7/1884)　　　Ann (8/18/1889).

In all, Denis Sullivan, Sr., fathered thirteen (13) children, all but three in Yonkers, NY. The subject of this study is Patrick.

Patrick was Denis' seventh child, whose mother was Sarah Duffy Sullivan.

Denis Sullivan, Sr., died on April 1, 1914 in Yonkers, NY.

Sarah Duffy Sullivan died in Yonkers, NY on May 26, 1923

As best as can be determined, Sarah and Denis Sullivan's family never reconciled with Patrick, his wife, or children.

Patrick Sullivan and Mary Carroll Sullivan had five children. The oldest were twins, Joseph and Vincent.

Of the five Sullivan children, only three (Joseph, John, Mary) had children.

Joseph's four children are;

Joseph, Jr., also called Junior (7/13/1922), became a Capuchin Friar and was known as Fr. Jordan.

Gloria (12/28/1923) became an Ursuline sister and was first known as Mother Mary Eileen before, again, being known as Sr. Gloria.

Roland (4/3/1929)

Janice known as Mrs. Janice DePiu (6/7/1931).

John's three children are;

Mary (6/27/1931) (Mrs. Mary Flinn),

Patricia (5/23/1934) (Patricia Drain)

John Jr. (3/29/1942).

Mary Sullivan Baldwin had one son, Joseph (8/30/1939.

As with all family trees, each of the Sullivan children had their own children who, subsequently, had their own children, and the list goes on adding branches upon branches. But the strength of the tree comes from its root and trunk. The roots of personal strength are clearly those of Bernard Carroll, Sr., and Mary (Nana) Carroll; The trunk being Mom Sullivan and Uncles John and Barney Carroll. We are the branches and leaves.

JOSEPH			VINCENT		JOH
MARY PHILLIPS					MARY "M

JOSEPH JR.	GLORIA	ROLAND	JANICE		MARY	PATRIC
FR. JORDAN	SR. GLORIA	BARBARA ROSS	HARRY DEPUY		DONALD FLINN	JOHN DRA

G CHILDREN	G CHILDREN		G CHILDREN	5 CHILDRE

10 GRANDCHILDREN	5 GRANDCHILDREN	6 GRANDCHILDREN	11 GRAND

1 GREAT-GRANDCHILD	2 GREA

AN   AND   MARY JANE CARROLL

HN
AE° MAXWELL

JOHN JR	
ELAINE Di COLA	THERESA DELL'OLIO

MARY
THOMAS BALDWIN

JOSEPH	
EVELYN WYCKOFF	MARIANNE DIGGINS

ARTHUR
ROSE MARSH

ROSE MARIE

N

2 CHILDREN

2 CHILDREN

1 CHILD

HILDREN   1 GRANDCHILD

2 GRANDCHILDREN

3 GRANDCHILDREN

F-GRANDCHILDREN

Bibliography

"American Historical Association". http://www.historians.org/

"American Heritage". http://americanheritage.com.

Ancestry. com

Army Records Ctr., Military.Archives.com

Bailey, Thomas A.; Lizabeth Cohen, and David M. Kennedy (2006). *The American Pageant: A History of the Republic* (13th ed.).

Bennett, William (2007). *America: The Last Best Hope*. ISBN 1595550550.

Blum, John M.; William S. McFeely, Edmund S. Morgan, Arthur M. Schlesinger, Jr., Kenneth M. Stampp, and C. Vann Woodward (1993).

Blum, John M.; William S. McFeely, Edmund S. Morgan, Arthur M. Schlesinger, Jr., Kenneth M. Stampp, and C. Vann Woodward (1985). *The National Experience: A History of the United States* (6th ed.). ISBN 0155656643

Carnes, Mark C., and John A. Garraty, *The American Nation: A History of the United States* (14th ed. 2011)

Clements, Kendrick A. (1992). *The Presidency of Woodrow Wilson*. University Press of Kansas. ISBN 0-7006-0524-X.

"Constitution of the United States". United States Senate. http://www.senate.gov/civics/constitution_item/constitution.htm#amendments.

Divine, Robert A. et al. *America Past and Present* (8th ed. 2011), university textbook.

Elizabeth Frost-Knappman and Kathryn Cullen-Dupont, *Women's Suffrage in America* (2004).

Family Archives 1880-1985.

Federal Census Bureau (1890-1930).

George Mowry, *The Era of Theodore Roosevelt and the Birth of Modern America, 1900–1912* (Harpers, 1954).

Jaap Jacobs, *The Colony of New Netherland: A Dutch Settlement in Seventeenth-Century America* (2nd ed. Cornell University Press; 2009).

Johnson, Paul (1999). *A History of the American People*. ISBN 0-06-093034-9

Johnston, Robert D. (2002). The Making of America: The History of the United States from 1492 to the Present. National Geographic. ISBN 0792269446

Johnston, Robert D. (2002). The Making of America: The History of the United States from 1492 to the Present. National Geographic.

Karen Morey Kennedy and Austin N. O'Brien (April 1983). "National Register of Historic Places Registration:Alexander Smith Carpet Mills Historic District". New York State Office of Parks, Recreation and Historic Preservation.

History of Woman Suffrage, Volume I by Susan B. (Susan Brownell) Anthony, Elizabeth Cady Stanton and Matilda Joslyn Gage).

"Library of Congress". http://www.loc.gov/index.html

Link, Arthur Stanley (1972). *Woodrow Wilson and the Progressive Era, 1910–1917*. HarperCollins. ISBN 006133023X

Longstar, American Cultural History, http:kclibrary.longstar.com

McNabb, James B. (2005). "Germany's Decision for Unrestricted Submarine Warfare and Its Impact on the U.S. Declaration of War".

Milkis, Sidney M.; Jerome M. Mileur (1999). *Progressivism and the New Democracy*. Amherst, MA: University of Massachusetts Press.

"National Register Information System". *National Register of Historic Places*. National Park Service. 2009-03-13.

"Population: 1790 to 1990" (PDF). United States Census Bureau. http://www.census.gov/population/censusdata/table-4.pdf

Roberts, Priscilla Mary and Spencer Tucker. *World War I: Encyclopedia*. ABC-CLIO.

Schweikart, Larry, and Dave Dougherty. *A Patriot's History of the Modern World, Vol. I: From America's Exceptional Ascent to the Atomic Bomb: 1898-1945; Vol. II: From the Cold War to the Age of Entitlement, 1945-2012* (2 vol. 2013).

"Tyler, The Creator Gets Odd In 'Yonkers'". Rapfix.mtv.com. 2011-02-11.

"U.S. Chronology World History Database". http://www.badley.info/history/USA.index.html

U. S. Department of State. "Outline of U.S. History".

U.S. Census Bureau. "Earliest Population Figures for American Cities". http://www.census.gov/population/www/documentation/twps0027/tab02.txt

Urofsky, Melvin I. (2000). *The American Presidents*. Taylor & Francis. ISBN 978-0-8153-2184-2

Westchester County Surrogates' Court, Yonkers, NY

Whitley, Peggy. "1900-1909." *American Cultural History*. Lone Star College-Kingwood, Library, 1999. Web. 7 Feb. 2011.

Whitley, Peggy. "1910-1919." *American Cultural History*. Lone Star College-Kingwood, Library, 1999. Web. 7 Feb. 2011.

Whitley, Peggy. "1920-1929." *American Cultural History*. Lone Star College-Kingwood, Library, 1999. Web. 7 Feb. 2011.

Wikipedia, Free Encyclopedia, www.wikipedia.org.

"WWW-VL: History: United States". http://vlib.iue.it/history/USA/

Yonkers Bureau of Vital Statistics, Yonkers, NY

Yonkers Herald – 1900-1925, Yonkers, NY

Yonkers Historical Society, Yonkers, NY

Yonkers Public Library, Yonkers, NY

Yonkers Record – 1900-1925, Yonkers, NY

"Yonkers (city), New York". *State & County QuickFacts*. U.S. Census Bureau.

"Yonkers (city), New York State & County QuickFacts". U.S. Census Bureau. Retrieved 2014-02-10.

Zinn, Howard (2003). *A People's History of the United States*. ISBN 0-06-052837-0

Made in the USA
Middletown, DE
28 September 2021